# Speed Learning

## A Cool System For Remembering The Dates And Meanings Of The Twelve Signs Of The Zodiac

### Print Edition

Includes 12 flash cards and audio to help you learn the system - see link at end of book

Sign up to our mailing list and get three free ebooks too!

See website for more details:

www.thecoldreadingcompany.co.uk

julian@thecoldreadingcompany.co.uk
**www.thecoldreadingcompany.co.uk**

**Other books in the 'Speed Learning' series
by Julian Moore**

Palmistry - Palm Readings In Your Own Words

Graphology - The Art Of Handwriting Analysis

Cartomancy - Fortune Telling With Playing Cards

The James Bond Cold Reading

Numerology - Numbers Past And Present With
The Lo-Shu Square

**www.thecoldreadingcompany.co.uk**

# CONTENTS

# Introduction

Most people know what their star sign is, whether they believe it has any significant or not. The twelve signs revolve around the twelve months of the year and each sign has a personality type associated with it, but even though there are only twelve of these signs many people find it extremely hard to remember them all.

Even more struggle to remember the meaning of each star sign, and remembering the dates that each sign falls on is something that most people never get to grips with.

Including me.

This book teaches the system I came up with to remember all this information. Hopefully by the time you've digested the contents of this book you'll be able to recall the names, dates and meanings of each and every star sign with ease. With a tiny bit of revision every now and again you should remember this information forever.

I have found that when books describe things for people to learn it is easy for readers to skip sections, even though the author has specifically asked for certain facts to be thought through and deliberated. To stop this from happening, and to encourage readers to properly engage with the material presented herein, I have given guidelines for the amount of time that each exercise should take.

I hope that by giving an indication of time and effort there will be less chance of speed reading and more likelihood of speed learning. The time required is quite minimal in the scheme of things, but learning is not magic; you can't learn something if you haven't thought about it properly, and this book is all about thinking things through and making connections.

You will probably have to read through this book a few times before you've got the whole system down, but I can't force you to learn. You have to put the time and effort in yourself. With a bit of luck you'll learn the names, dates and meanings of each star sign quicker than you ever thought possible.

```
WHAT YOU CAN IMAGINE,
   YOU CAN REMEMBER.
```

## Registration

At the end of this book is a registration link from which you can download the flash cards and audio, designed to help you get this information into your head as quickly as possible. Print out the flash cards onto index cards using your home printer and use them in tandem with this text or when you're out and about for a quick bit of revision, and listen to the audio in the car or on your favourite music device for a quick blast of background learning. Without using the flash cards and audio you simply won't learn as fast; when it comes to absorbing new information quickly, you're better off coming at it from as many angles as possible.

# Overview

**A brief rundown on what to expect from this book**

This book is mostly about creating strong mental images. If you have any kind of imagination this system should work for you.

People often talk about star signs belonging to a certain month, although each star sign ends around the third week of each. By assigning each star sign a month and a 'switch over' date you can keep the traditional idea of one sign per month and use a simple system to remember when each sign changes to the next.

By combining strong mental images for each month and star sign it's pretty easy to remember which goes with which. And by combining these visualisations with each sign's character type you can not only learn their names, dates and meanings in a very short time; you'll have a strong framework to build upon should you go on to further study.

# The Month Images

**In this first chapter we learn to create a strong mental image for each month**

There are twelve months of the year and twelve signs of the zodiac. As we are going to be working with mental images throughout this book we need to create a visualisation for each month so we can recall them instantly. Unlike the signs of the zodiac, the months of the year are fairly abstract and don't actually 'look' like anything, but we can make them more stimulating by creating a mental image for each of them, such as the idea of Mayonnaise for the month of May.

Here's the list of months and their associated images. See if you can figure out why I have chosen each one:

January - Jam
February - Brew
March - Marsh
April - Pill
May - Mayonnaise
June - Tune
July - Lie
August - Gust
September - Scepter
October - Octopus
November - No
December - Dismember

It's all fairly simple but some images are a little more obvious than others:

JAM sounds like the start of JANuary, so you have the idea of jam, in a pot or spread over something

BREW sounds like the second part of feBRUary so there is the idea of beer, perhaps in a glass or jug

MARSH sounds like MARCH which is fairly straightforward, some kind of boggy landscape

PILL sounds like the end of aPRIL, and could refer to some kind of headache tablet

MAYONNAISE of course starts with MAY so this is easy to remember, a simple jar of mayonnaise for example

TUNE sounds almost identical to JUNE, so you have the idea of whistling harmonies

LIE is based on the end sound of the month juLY, the idea of a pair of crossed fingers to represent lying

GUST is the end sound of auGUST, the idea of a gust of wind

SCEPTER is based on the start sound of SEPTember, a scepter being a long ornate staff held by kings

NO is quite simply the start of the word NOvember, and is the idea of a warning, such as a 'keep out' or 'no entry' sign

DISMEMBER sounds almost exactly like DECEMBER, a rather gruesome lack of legs or arms

Even reading through this just once you'll be amazed how much of it you can recall, but let's get down to fixing this information in our minds for good.

Like all of the learning exercises in this book, I want you to read the following list of months and associated images SLOWLY. Each time you read a month and it's associated image, create a visualisation of the word as vividly as you can in your mind, then move on to the next one. You may want to stare into space, or close your eyes while you imagine each of them. Take your time, there's no hurry; what is important is you give each month and associated image enough time to sink in.

**Top Tip:** *Don't worry too much if you think nothing is happening or you're somehow 'doing it wrong'. You're going to be asked to do exercises like this throughout this book, so carry on regardless. You might think you're not learning anything, but keep reading and repeating and you'll be amazed how quickly you can digest all of this.*

Here's the list. Repeat each one in your mind a few times before moving on to the next.

**EXERCISE ONE - LEARNING - One minute total, five seconds each, repeat two or three times**

*Remember to repeat each one in your mind before moving to the next one*

January - Jam - JAMuary - a pot of jam

February - Brew - feBREWary - a beer in a glass

March - Marsh - MARSCH - a marshy bog

April - Pill - aPRIL - a headache tablet

May - Mayonnaise - MAYonnaise - a jar of mayonnaise

June - Tune - TJUNE - whistling, harmonies

July - Lie - juLIE - a fib, crossed fingers

August - Gust - auGUST - a big gust of wind

September - Scepter - SCEPTember - an ornate staff

October - Octopus - OCTOpus - an eight legged sea creature

November - No - NOvember - a warning, no entry sign

December - Dismember - DECmEMBER - chopped off legs

Now read through the list out loud before you move on. Don't forget to visualise each one - five seconds each!

Once you've done that, let's try the next exercise without looking at the previous list to see if you can recite it from memory.

**EXERCISE TWO - RECALL - One minute total, five seconds each, repeat two or three times**

*Do these ones in your head first*
January goes with ...
February goes with ....
March goes with .....
April goes with ...
May goes with ..........
June goes with ....
July goes with ....
August goes with ....
September goes with .......
October goes with .......
November goes with .........
December goes with .........

I think you'll be quite impressed how many of them you can remember, if not all of them.

Try the last exercise again but this time out loud, making a note of the months that slow you down.

You've got to be pretty honest with yourself here, and throughout the rest of the book. If you are finding this pretty easy then move on, but if you are slightly unsure of some months take the time to go over them again.

Once you think you can remember most of the months and associated images without too much fuss, try this next exercise by saying out loud the months associated with each of these ideas.

**EXERCISE THREE - RECALL - One minute total, five seconds each, repeat two or three times**

*Remember you need to say these ones out loud*

Gust is for ......
Tune is for ....
Lie is for ....
Scepter is for .........
Dismember is for ........
Brew is for ........
Pill is for .....
Mayonnaise is for ...
Octopus is for .......
No is for ........
Marsh is for .....
Jam is for .......

Read through the above list out loud again before you move on, filling in the month for each image.

The idea here is we're doing things in reverse by thinking of a mental image first and then calling out its associated month. The similarities in the sounds of months and images should be enough for you to recall the months fairly easily. For instance, as soon as I think of the word Marsh I know it's associated with the month March, as soon as I think of the word Jam I immediately think of January. Make sure you see each image in your mind's eye as vividly as possible.

*Top Tip: If you find that you're still having problems then you simply need a little more practice. Try writing the months and images down on paper, or recite them while you go about your everyday business. Make your visualisations as strong as possible and don't be afraid to spend a good few seconds imprinting the months and images of each one in your mind.*

Do not leave this chapter until you can remember the months and their images, it should take you no longer than ten to fifteen minutes. In the next section we're going to learn how to put this system to good use.

Only when you really think you've got your head around this chapter should you turn to the next.

# The Star Sign Images

**This chapter focuses on creating a strong mental image for each star sign**

Here is a list of the twelve signs of the zodiac, with their names and visual descriptions. Don't simply glance down this list; take the time to think about each sign. This first exercise isn't too intensive, it's just a way to familiarise yourself with everything.

See if you can notice any similarities between the name of each star sign and their visual description. Repeat each one out loud a few times before moving on to the next one. As you do so, just think about what these star signs mean to you and take note of the images they conjure up in your own mind.

**EXERCISE FOUR - LEARNING - One minute, five seconds each, repeat once**

*Don't forget to read these out loud*

Capricorn - The Goat *
Aquarius - The Water Bearer
Pisces - The Fish
Aries - The Ram
Taurus - The Bull
Gemini - The Twins
Cancer - The Crab
Leo - The Lion
Virgo - The Virgin
Libra - The Scales
Scorpio - The Scorpion
Sagittarius - The Centaur **

*\* Capricorn is actually half goat half fish, but I always think of it as half goat half mermaid*
*\*\* Sagittarius is a Centaur, half horse half man usually bearing a bow and arrow, also known as The Archer*

Read through the above list out loud once again before you move on.

Now let's create a much stronger mental image for each star sign based on their description. Spend at least ten seconds visualising each one of these signs. Close your eyes if you have to, and try to add as much colour and attention to detail as you can to each mental image.

*Top Tip:* *There is not a word wasted in these descriptions so please visualise everything that is mentioned; grassy fields, sandy beaches, flaming arrows, the lot! Every word has a purpose and you'll learn why later in the book!*

**EXERCISE FIVE - LEARNING - Two minutes, ten seconds each, repeat twice**

*Visualise each one of these as hard as you can!*

CAPRICORN - The Goat - Imagine a goat with a white beard standing in a grassy field

AQUARIUS - The Water Bearer - Imagine a beautiful princess pouring water through the air into a lake from a vase

PISCES - The Fish - Imagine two playful fish swimming in the sea

ARIES - The Ram - Imagine an angry white ram with fiery eyes and curly horns

TAURUS - The Bull - Imagine a strong headed bull in a fenced field

GEMINI - The Twins - Imagine two identical young twins holding hands in the air

CANCER - The Crab - Imagine a big red crab on a sandy beach

15

LEO - The Lion - Imagine a great lion with a fiery mane surveying its territory

VIRGO - The Virgin - Imagine an innocent young girl in a flowery field

LIBRA - The Scales - Imagine an empty pair of scales weighing nothing but air

SCORPIO - The Scorpion - Imagine a scorpion scuttling about on the sand near an oasis

SAGITTARIUS - The Centaur - Imagine a centaur firing a flaming arrow from a bow

Read through the above list once again before you move on. Don't forget to visualise each one as vividly as you can!

***Top Tip:*** *If you find you get Capricorn and Aries confused as they're fairly similar, just remember Capricorn is all about the goatee beard, and Aries is all about the curly horns. And why does the ram have fiery eyes? Because he's been ramming into things!*

Finding it hard to spend ten seconds on each one? Try first seeing each one in your mind's eye as a painting. Then imagine walking into the painting where it becomes three dimensional. Walk around the image, and try making it more like a movie. See the water running, the fish swimming - imagine you are actually there. Be creative. Take your time doing this; what you can imagine, you can remember.

Here's another thing to try. Do the exercises again but this time incorporate the name of each star sign into the picture. Perhaps you can see each star sign as a playing card with the name of each one printed at the bottom? Or how about seeing each one as a framed oil painting with the name of each one emblazoned on the frame itself? Or how about imagining each star sign as if you're watching them on music television, the name of each sign displayed at the bottom of the screen?

It doesn't matter what you do, as long as you do something that requires some creative mental effort on your part. Play with the images, spin them around in your mind, come at them from as many angles as you can think of. None of this is wasted time; it's going to be the difference between you remembering things vaguely or remembering things forever.

*Top Tip: Enjoy your daydreaming; the mental effort you spend thinking about these ideas is the glue you need to remember them. No mental effort, no recall.*

Don't forget to do the above exercise at least twice. You may not think you're going to remember the mental pictures that you're creating for yourself, but we are going to be revisiting them again and again, adding more detail each time. By the time you get to the end of this book you'll have a hard time forgetting them.

Now let's see if we can recall a few of these new memories with just the literal description of each sign. I've mixed them up a bit so you're going to have to recall them at random.

## EXERCISE SIX - RECALL - One minute, five seconds each

*Remember to give yourself time to recreate each mental image*

I am The Scorpion. Revisit my mental image.
I am The Virgin. Revisit my mental image.
I am The Crab. Revisit my mental image.
I am The Bull. Revisit my mental image.
I am The Fish. Revisit my mental image.
I am The Goat. Revisit my mental image.
I am The Centaur. Revisit my mental image.
I am The Scales. Revisit my mental image.
I am The Lion. Revisit my mental image.

We are The Twins. Revisit my mental image.
I am The Water Bearer. Revisit my mental image.
I am The Ram. Revisit my mental image.

How did you get on? If you found it a bit too hard simply read through this chapter again. Make a note of the signs you're having the most problems with and spend a little more time visualising them. As I've said before, if you're not brutally honest with yourself about which signs you're having problems with you will struggle later on, so don't continue unless you're fairly happy with your ability to conjure up each of these images up in your mind.

If you're able to recall these signs more often than not, let's see how well you do at connecting the name of each sign with their mental image. Although we're going to address the actual names of the signs in the next chapter, it's worth seeing just how much has sunk in so far.

**EXERCISE SEVEN - RECALL - One minute, five seconds each**

*Close your eyes as you recall each one if it helps!*

Recall the mental image for Aries. Describe it out loud.
Recall the mental image for Aquarius. Describe it out loud.
Recall the mental image for Leo. Describe it out loud.
Recall the mental image for Libra. Describe it out loud.
Recall the mental image for Sagittarius. Describe it out loud.
Recall the mental image for Capricorn. Describe it out loud.
Recall the mental image for Pisces. Describe it out loud.
Recall the mental image for Taurus. Describe it out loud.
Recall the mental image for Cancer. Describe it out loud.
Recall the mental image for Virgo. Describe it out loud.
Recall the mental image for Scorpio. Describe it out loud.
Recall the mental image for Gemini. Describe it out loud.

If you have some prior knowledge of star signs then you may find you have no difficulty in connecting the names of each sign with their mental image. However if you're slightly new to all of this the next chapter will give you some further tips to help you connect the names of the signs with their descriptions.

If you're feeling quite comfortable with what you've learned in this chapter, turn to the next one. If not, perhaps take a short break before reading through this chapter again.

# Star Sign Names

**Here are some useful tips to help you remember the names of the signs of the zodiac**

*If you're already familiar with the the names of the signs of the zodiac then you can skip this section*

You might have found it quite easy to create the visualisations in the last chapter, but remembering the actual names of each star sign can seem a little abstract if you've never been exposed to them before. There's a good chance you know the names of most of them already, but it's not my place to assume and I have to write this book as if you know absolutely nothing. It's worth reading through these tips, but in practice you'll probably only need a few of them for those harder to remember signs.

**AQUARIUS The Water Bearer**
Clue: The clue is in the name - AQUA - rius

**PISCES The Fish**
Clue: Pi - SEAS - Fish swim in seas, right?

**ARIES The Ram**
Clue: AIR - ies - The Ram is fluffy like a cloud (air)

**TAURUS The Bull**
Clue: The bull TORE - US a hole in our pants with its horns

**GEMINI The Twins**
Clue: ge - MINI is the two small (mini) twins

**CANCER The Crab**
Clue: The crab is dark pink, like skin CANCER - crab spent too long in the sun?

## LEO The Lion
Clue: Leo the lion - possibly the easiest star sign to remember!

## VIRGO The Virgin
Clue: VIRG - o  VIRG - in

## LIBRA The Scales
Clue: Li - BRA - A ladies bra does a kind of balancing act. Now there's a mental image...

## SCORPIO The Scorpion
Clue: Scorpio - N - easy!

That's ten of the twelve star signs. The first and the last have the most abstract names and I find are the hardest to remember for that reason. You may well find my clues for these unsatisfactory. Please feel free to come up with your own absurd connections for these last two signs if you find mine somewhat lacking!

## SAGITTARIUS The Centaur
Clue: Saggy Teary Ass - The Centaur is a bit old and weepy and has a donkeys backside!

## CAPRICORN The Goat
Clue: Imagine a goat eating CORN on the island of CAPRI

You may find some of the clues more helpful than others. If you have difficulties remembering one or two of these then you should spend a little time creating your own clues so you don't forget them. There's nothing so useful as a memory aid you yourself have created!

Let's try an easy exercise to see if you can remember any of this.

## EXERCISE EIGHT - RECALL - One minute, five seconds each

*Try and remember the clue for each one!*

What is The Ram called?
What are The Twins called?
What is The Lion called?
What are The Scales called?
What is The Water Bearer called?
What is The Fish called?
What is The Bull called?
What is The Crab called?
What is The Virgin called?
What is The Scorpion called?
What is The Goat called?
What is The Centaur called?

Like most people you probably find that you can remember the names of most of these pretty easily, with three or four of them being a little bit harder to recall. Make a note of the ones you can't remember that well and take the time to revise these tips, and possibly come up with your own.

As long as you feel reasonably comfortable with the names of each star sign, let's move on to the next chapter.

# Months And Signs

**Let's have a quick recap of the month images before we combine everything we've learned so far**

Read this list out loud again just like you did back in chapter one.

**EXERCISE NINE - RECAP - One minute total, five seconds each, repeat two or three times**

*Out loud! Speak up!*

January - Jam
February - Brew
March - Marsh
April - Pill
May - Mayonnaise
June - Tune
July - Lie
August - Gust
September - Scepter
October - Octopus
November - No
December - Dismember

Read through the above list out loud again before you move on, and then see if you can run through it again without looking.

The month images should be sinking in by now. We're now going to combine the month images with the star signs through a series of new combined visualisations.

Here are the months and their images alongside each star sign. Have a casual read through this list, thinking about how you can connect each month's image with each star sign.

January - Jam - Capricorn - The Goat

February - Brew - Aquarius - The Water Bearer

March - Marsh - Pisces - The Fish

April - Pill - Aries - The Ram

May - Mayonnaise - Taurus - The Bull

June - Tune - Gemini - The Twins

July - Lie - Cancer - The Crab

August - Gust - Leo - The Lion

September - Scepter - Virgo - The Virgin

October - Octopus - Libra - The Scales

November - No - Scorpio - The Scorpion

December - Dismember - Sagittarius - The Centaur

This can look a bit abstract with the months, month images and star signs all together, but with a little thought we can link these ideas up so we'll find them hard to forget.

The idea is that if we can recall one, we can recall the other. For instance, if we can remember a goat (Capricorn) with a jammy beard, we can remember January. And if we can remember that May goes with mayonnaise, we can remember a bull (Taurus) eating mayonnaise.

With this in mind, imagine these next examples as vividly as you can, creating a strong mental image for each one. As with the previous visualisations you may need to close your eyes and really concentrate, but I promise you it's worth taking the time to do this properly and it still only comes down to a matter of minutes.

**EXERCISE TEN - LEARNING - Two to three minutes total, five to ten seconds each, repeat at least twice**

*This bit is really important so you need to imagine each one as vividly as possible!*

CAPRICORN: Imagine a goat with a white beard covered in JAM standing in a grassy field

AQUARIUS: Imagine a beautiful princess pouring BEER through the air into a lake from a large vase

PISCES: Imagine two playful fish swimming in a MARSH

ARIES: Imagine an angry white ram with fiery eyes taking a PILL for his migraine

TAURUS: Imagine a strong headed bull in a fenced field licking MAYONNAISE out of a jar

GEMINI: Imagine two identical young twins holding hands in the air whistling a TUNE together

CANCER: Imagine a big red crab on a sandy beach telling a LIE (crossing its claws as if it's fibbing)

LEO: Imagine a great lion with a fiery mane blown by a GUST of wind as it surveys its territory

VIRGO: Imagine an innocent young girl in a flowery field holding a SCEPTER

LIBRA: Imagine an empty pair of scales weighing nothing but air held by an OCTOPUS

SCORPIO: Imagine a scorpion scuttling about on the sand near an oasis with a NO entry sign

SAGITTARIUS: Imagine a centaur with no legs (DISMEMBER) firing a flaming arrow from a bow

Once you've got to the end of this list, go back and re-visualise each of them one more time.

And then, once you've gone through this process twice, try and forget everything. You'll understand why later.

(Feel free to have a third go around if you like, but don't forget that once you're finished I want you to try and forget everything you've just imagined!)

Of course, forgetting everything you've just imagined is almost impossible, simply because it's very hard to forget things you've put the time into imagining. The main problem with people who say they have a bad memory is not that they can't recall things that they've learned, it's that they've not put enough creative effort into learning things in the first place.

**Top Tip:** *If your head is hurting from doing all that visualisation, take a break. You'll be amazed how much you can remember hours or days from now, even though you've only done these exercises a few times.*

Now let's see if this has been of any use. Here are some questions, see how well you do:

**EXERCISE ELEVEN - RECALL - One minute total, about five seconds each**

*See the object in your mind and let the greater picture come to you - if shouldn't take too much effort*

Which star sign has a beard covered in jam?
Which star sign is pouring beer into a lake?

Which star sign is swimming in a marsh?
Which star sign is taking a headache pill?
Which star sign is licking a jar of mayonnaise?
Which star sign is whistling a tune in harmony?
Which star sign is telling a lie?
Which star sign is having its hair blown by a gust of wind?
Which star sign is holding a scepter?
Which star sign is an octopus holding?
Which star sign is holding a no entry sign?
Which star sign has its legs missing?

You may find that you can recall the visual image in your mind for many of these, but you can't recall the name of the star sign itself. Not to worry. Mark down the star signs whose names you find more difficult than others and have a go at re-visualising them before having another go at the list.

What should become apparent is that some of the signs are extremely well matched with the words given for each month:

*February has the word BREW so it's easy to remember that it's Aquarius The Water Bearer pouring beer instead of water*

*March has the word MARSH so it's obvious that Pisces The Fish should be swimming in it*

*November simply has the word NO, if there's one sign you shouldn't go near it's Scorpio The Scorpion!*

Now go back to the start of this chapter and read it all over again if you haven't already, repeating the exercises before moving on.

We're now going to try the previous questions but in a different order.

**EXERCISE TWELVE - RECALL - One minute, about five seconds each**

*Don't stress out too much about answering these questions, just relax and let the answers come to you*

Which star sign has its legs missing?
Which star sign is pouring beer into a lake?
Which star sign is holding a scepter?
Which star sign is an octopus holding?
Which star sign is swimming in a marsh?
Which star sign has a white beard covered in jam?
Which star sign is taking a headache pill?
Which star sign is licking a jar of mayonnaise?
Which star sign is having its hair blown by a gust of wind?
Which star sign is holding a no entry sign?
Which star sign is whistling a harmonious tune?
Which star sign is telling a lie?

By this point you should be getting the hang of this. When you visualise one of the month words its associated star sign should be arriving in your mind pretty much simultaneously. You now have a combined mental image for each sign; they're one and the same.

This is one of the most important chapters in this book as it combines everything we have learned so far. Have another read through it if you need to before moving on to the next chapter. Don't forget that the flash cards and audio can really help you learn this stuff a lot quicker; it's worth spending the time printing off the flash cards and getting the audio somewhere you can listen to it!

# The 23rd Day Premise

**Now we're going to start learning how to calculate people's star signs with 87% accuracy**

In a perfect world, each star sign would fall exactly on each month of the year and by simply knowing the month someone was born in you could know their star sign. Unfortunately it's not that simple, but do not despair as the system in this book takes care of that.

Most people learn that each month corresponds to one star sign, yet each sign ends around the third week of each month. For instance, people who know a little about horoscopes might say that Capricorns are born in January which is only partly true; once you get past the 20th of January you're into the next sign along, Aquarius. So most people think about star signs as 'belonging' to the months they have the most weeks in, even though that's not quite accurate.

Each star sign starts between the 19th and the 23rd of each month (I call this 'The Cusp Zone') and this region is the cut-off point for us to know whether a person's star sign is taken from the month their birthday falls in or the next month along. Generally speaking, if someone is born towards the end of a month their star sign takes that of the next month. People whose birthdays fall in or around The Cusp Zone are said to be born 'on the cusp' as their birthday falls close enough to another sign to inherit some of its traits.

It should be noted that only one star sign actually starts on the 19th of any month (Pisces in February) but all the other star signs start in the twenties from the 20th to the 23rd of each month.

For now, and before we learn to calculate star sign dates with 100% accuracy, we're going to simply pretend that ALL star signs start on the 23rd of the month, something I call 'The 23rd

Day Premise'. By falsely using the 23rd as the start day for every star sign in every month we can get an overall feel for the system before we take things further.

So just for now, our not-quite-accurate star sign dates will look like this:

23rd December to 22nd January - Capricorn
23rd January to 22nd February - Aquarius
23rd February to 22nd March - Pisces
23rd March to 22nd April - Aries
23rd April to 22nd May - Taurus
23rd May to 22nd June - Gemini
23rd June to 22nd July - Cancer
23rd July to 22nd August - Leo
23rd August to 22nd September - Virgo
23rd September to 22nd October - Libra
23rd October to 22nd November - Scorpio
23rd November to 22rd December - Sagittarius

As you can see, Capricorn mostly belongs to January, but starts at the end of December. Aquarius mostly belongs to February, but starts at the end of January, etc. All star signs end in the months they inhabit the most.

With so many dates this can still appear a little confusing, so let's just concentrate on the months each sign has the most days in:

January - Capricorn
February - Aquarius
March - Pisces
April - Aries
May - Taurus
June - Gemini
July - Cancer
August - Leo
September - Virgo
October - Libra

November - Scorpio
December - Sagittarius

For now this is all you need to know, and you only have to remember that each sign starts on the 23rd of the month. Capricorn 'belongs' to January, Aquarius 'belongs' to February etc.

## Close But No Cigar

Now let's use The 23rd Day Premise and learn to remember the signs as if they ALL started on the 23rd of each month.

If all star signs started on the 23rd of their respective months, we'd know this much:

1. If someone's birthday falls before the 23rd of any given month, their star sign is from the same month

2. If someone's birthday falls on or after the 23rd of any given month, their star sign is from the next month

**For instance:**

* If someone told you they were born on October 2nd, you'd know straight away that their star sign was from the same month

* If someone told you they were born on December 28th, you'd know straight away that their star sign is from the next month, January

* If someone told you they were born on April 18th, you'd know straight away that their star sign was from the same month

* If someone told you they were born on July 24th, you'd know straight away that their star sign is from the next month, August

* If someone told you they were born on January 5th, you'd know straight away that their star sign was from the same month

So the rule for remembering which month to use for someone's star sign is:

**Use the current month's star sign before the 23rd, otherwise use the next month's sign.**

By knowing this, and with what we're already learned to visualise, we can now instantly calculate anyone's star sign from their birth date. Well, nearly, because by pretending that each start sign starts on the 23rd of each month we can only be 87% accurate, simply because the signs vary their start dates between the 19th and the 23rd of each month as we have discussed.

Although later in the book we will learn how to be 100% accurate, let's work with being 87% accurate for now while we get a feel for how this all works.

# How to put The 23rd Day Premise into practice:

1. Find out someone's date of birth

2. If the DAY they were born is before the 23rd of the month, they take the star sign from the same month; otherwise the next

3. Think of the month word for the relevant month and you'll immediately know what star sign they are

**That's it!**

**Example One:** Someone tells you they were born on the 10th of July. They were born on the 10th which is before the 23rd so you keep the month. The month image for July is LIE and you immediately see Cancer The Crab lying with its claws crossed. The person is a Cancer.

**Example Two:** Someone tells you they were born on the 25th of January. The 25th is after the 23rd so you use the next month, February. You think of the month image for February which is BREW. The moment you think of brew you can see Aquarius The Water Bearer pouring beer into a lake. The person is an Aquarius.

That sounds quite lengthy, but it can go very fast indeed with a small amount of practice. The moment you have the correct month image you jump straight to the associated visualisation and see the relevant star sign. The important thing you have to remember is to go forwards a month if the day the person was born on falls on or after the 23rd. As about three quarters of all star signs start before the 23rd you'll only be going forward to the next month roughly a quarter of the time.

Let's test how good you are at this. Answer these questions as if every star sign started on the 23rd of the month. What is each person's star sign? Don't forget, go forward a month if the day is on or after the 23rd of the month, otherwise use the month you're on. And then remember the word that goes with the month you are left with.

## EXERCISE THIRTEEN - RECALL - One minute total, five seconds each

*Take your time, it will get easier with practice!*

I was born on the 24th of January. What star sign am I?
I was born on the 5th February. What star sign am I?
I was born on the 30th March. What star sign am I?
I was born on the 15th April. What star sign am I?
I was born on the 2nd May. What star sign am I?
I was born on the 9th June. What star sign am I?
I was born on the 24th July. What star sign am I?
I was born on the 1st August. What star sign am I?
I was born on the 25th September. What star sign am I?
I was born on the 20th October. What star sign am I?
I was born on the 30th November. What star sign am I?
I was born on the 4th December. What star sign am I?

After attempting those twelve questions you should be getting a feel for how the star signs overlap the end of one month and the majority of the next. You should also be getting the hang of working out fairly rapidly whether you need to go forward a month or not.

Let's do things in reverse just once to make sure we're joining everything up properly in our minds. To do the next exercise you're going to have to think of the mental image you have of a star sign, see the month word in that image, and then convert it back into its actual month.

**EXERCISE FOURTEEN - RECALL - Two minutes total, ten seconds each**

*This is a bit easier than the last exercise, but still good practice!*

I'm a Capricorn. What month does my star sign start in?
I'm a Sagittarius. What month does my star sign start in?
I'm a Scorpio. What month does my star sign start in?
I'm an Aries. What month does my star sign start in?
I'm a Pisces. What month does my star sign start in?
I'm an Aquarius. What month does my star sign start in?
I'm a Cancer. What month does my star sign start in?
I'm a Gemini. What month does my star sign start in?
I'm a Taurus. What month does my star sign start in?
I'm a Libra. What month does my star sign start in?
I'm a Virgo. What month does my star sign start in?
I'm a Leo. What month does my star sign start in?

Make sure you're pretty happy with The 23rd Day Premise before you move on. You may need to run through it a couple of times but it's important as it lays the foundations of what is to come.

# The Cusp Zone Fluff

**A small chapter on dealing with The Cusp Zone and The 23rd Day Premise**

*If you're keen to put what you've learned so far into practice and don't mind the odd mistake, read this chapter*

When someone is born outside The Cusp Zone (before the 19th or on or after the 23rd) you have nothing to worry about and your calculations will always be correct. It's only when people are born INSIDE The Cusp Zone that there's a chance for error.

However, you'll still be correct some of the time as four signs of the zodiac start on the 23rd of the month, and even if you're wrong you'll only ever be one month away from the correct star sign.

It's still worth using the 23rd Day Premise when you're getting started, even if there's a slim chance of failure. Better to practice this now as you'll learn how to be more accurate later in the book. Here is how you can make a comeback if you find that you are wrong when dealing with someone born in The Cusp Zone.

## Fluffing The Cusp Using The 23rd Day Premise

If someone tells you their date of birth and it's in The Cusp Zone (19th - 23rd) you can pause and say 'How interesting, you're on the cusp!'. This immediately makes you sound like you know what you're talking about, and gives you a little more time to think.

You then tell them their star sign by using The 23rd Day Premise, and quite often you'll be correct. But what if you're wrong?

Similar to the calculations we've already learnt to do, people born in The Cusp Zone take either the sign for their month or the next month. However, if they're not one, they're the other:

*If you are wrong and you DIDN'T go forward a month, then DO; their star sign is from the next month*

*If you are wrong and you DID go forward a month, then DON'T; their star sign is from their original month*

**Lucky Example:** Someone tells you that they were born on the 21st of October. You pause, you're in The Cusp Zone! 'How interesting, you're on the cusp!' you exclaim. The 21st is before the 23rd so you stay with October and remember the OCTOPUS holding the scales for LIBRA. You tell the person she's a Libra. You're correct! Phew, that was lucky.

**Unlucky Example:** Someone tells you that they were born on the 22nd of December. You pause, you're in The Cusp Zone! 'How interesting, you're on the cusp!' you exclaim. The 22nd is before the 23rd so you stay with December. You tell the person she's a Sagittarius. Oh no, you're wrong - but you can come back with the right sign almost immediately by using the next month of January and remembering the JAM on the goat's beard for CAPRICORN. You apologise and tell the person she's a Capricorn. Second time lucky and you're correct, but a good recovery and you still look like you know what you're talking about.

As you can see from these two examples it's incredibly easy to go forward or back a month, and because you already know if someone is born in The Cusp Zone you can take a little more time to get ready to switch signs should you get it wrong.

Around 13% of people are born in The Cusp Zone, and if you use The 23rd Day Premise for those people, you'll still be right a third of the time. So as you can see it's definitely worth having a stab at it anyway.

# Star Sign Meanings

**A new method for remembering the meanings of star signs**

Remembering the meanings of each star sign can be just as problematic as remembering their dates, but for entirely different reasons. The difficulty with connecting a series of character traits to a star sign is that they can be vague, subtle and sometimes quite similar to one another. As star signs are largely archetypal my solution is to attach a suitable fictional character to each sign, rather than try and remember a long list of hard to remember attributes.

Let's take Scorpio as an example. Here are some traditional meanings, both positive and negative, for Scorpio:

## SCORPIO

*Positive Traits: Secretive, powerful, domineering, resistant, intuitive, asserted, charismatic, magnetic, strong-willed, perspicacious, passionate, creative, independent, vigorous, generous, loyal, hard-working, persevering, untamable, possessive, cunning, ambitious, sexual, proud, intense, competitive.*

*Negative Traits: Aggressive, destructive, stubborn, anxious, tyrannical, perverse, sadistic, violent, self-centered, complex, jealous.*

Reading through that list of attributes for Scorpio is all very well, but attaching these ideas to Scorpio in a memorable way is almost impossible as there just aren't enough mental hooks. This is why so many people, even those who've been interested in horoscopes for years, reach for their star sign book so very often; they simply can't remember the numerous character traits for each sign and need to continually reference what each one actually means.

The preferred career paths of each star sign are a lot easier to remember. Here are some of the types of career that Scorpios tend to be attracted to:

**Preferred Scorpio career paths:** *Gynecologist, psychiatrist, detective, police, the military, stockbroker, asset manager.*

I'm sure you'd agree that remembering a few of these career paths is a lot easier than remembering a sprawling list of character traits.

If we choose just three of these likely career paths for the Scorpio such as psychiatry, detective and police work, what can we say about the Scorpio character? Intuitive, charismatic, magnetic, strong-willed, creative, independent, loyal, hard-working, persevering, cunning, ambitious and competitive all fit the psychiatrist / detective / police mentality. By knowing each star sign's most likely career paths it's fairly easy to work backwards and describe their character traits based on these professions.

Fictional characters are largely archetypal as they are constructed to act and behave in certain ways and don't suffer as much from the cultural and geographical boundaries of 'real' people. This makes them ideal to attach to the visualisations we created in the first half of this book, one character for each star sign, choosing characters that encompass each star sign's professions as broadly as possible.

Going back to the Scorpion's preferred career paths, I think it's safe to say that not many people would like to describe what a gynecologist does in any great detail, and there aren't many fictional stockbrokers or asset managers that spring to mind in the world of literature or popular culture. But psychiatrist detective policemen? We're spoilt for choice! Let's choose the the most famous fictional detective of them all - Sherlock Holmes, the London sleuth of 22b Baker Street, renowned for his intuition and deduction skills. If we attach the idea of

Sherlock Holmes to Scorpio in our minds, we'll never be stuck for something to say about a Scorpio.

So what can we say about Sherlock Holmes? He is certainly cunning. He has an amazing ability to work things out and to see 'what's what'. He is incredibly intuitive and doesn't miss a thing. This can make him seem quite insular at times but he's not being rude; he's thinking. He never gives up and sees things through to their logical conclusion. This can make him appear quite cold but in fact he's quite a romantic character and is prone to acts of spontaneity (such as picking up his violin and playing it while he thinks!) He's competitive and loves a challenge, and is rarely proven wrong. He uses his quite considerable charm to get what he wants but this never feels forced, although sometimes it can come across as arrogant. He can be a very loyal friend (as he was to Dr Watson) but would prefer to have the upper hand in a relationship as he is somewhat independent in mind as well as action. He works hard and plays hard and doesn't see much of a distinction between the two. People are drawn to him but as he is quite a complex character; some people may feel that they've never really got to know him, even if they've been friends for years.

In the previous paragraph I have expanded on the central theme of Sherlock Holmes, which in itself describes a large part of the Scorpio character. I have not had to refer to any list of traits to do this but have simply used the character of Sherlock Holmes as a springboard to enable me to remember a large majority of the personality traits that make up a Scorpio. Of course Sherlock Holmes doesn't encompass everything there is to know about the Scorpio personality but it's a great starting point, and more details can be added later.

By applying the same visualisation techniques used in the first half of this book it is very simple to attach an appropriate fictional character to each star sign. For each sign I have chosen three preferred professions, and with those in mind I have decided upon a fictional character that I feel encompasses as much of the idea of each star sign as possible. You may not be familiar with some of my choices and you may decide to choose your own as some signs lend themselves to fictional characters more than others (Scorpio is one of the better ones). Either way, the next section will give you a framework to build upon and you can choose different characters that you are more comfortable with where you see fit.

# The Twelve Characters

Here are the twelve characters I have chosen for the star signs. Browse the list and see how many you know.

CAPRICORN - Atticus Finch from 'To Kill A Mockingbird'

AQUARIUS - Communications Officer Uhura from 'Star Trek'

PISCES - Captain Jack Sparrow from 'Pirates Of The Caribbean'

ARIES - Willy Wonka from 'Willy Wonka And The Chocolate Factory'

TAURUS - Chef from 'South Park'

GEMINI - John Keating from 'Dead Poets Society'

CANCER - Lovejoy from the BBC TV series 'Lovejoy'

LEO - Yoda from 'Star Wars'

VIRGO - Miss Moneypenny from the Bond films

LIBRA - Edna Mode from 'The Incredibles'

SCORPIO - Sherlock Holmes from the books by Sir Arthur Conan Doyle

SAGITTARIUS - Indiana Jones from 'Raiders Of The Lost Ark'

There now follows a more detailed explanation for each star sign, revisiting our original visualisations and combining them with these new characters and ideas. There is also a list of positive traits for each sign so you can see the broader picture for each one. While you're reading through them, have a think about how your visualisations are going to expand to accommodate these new ideas and characters.

For each sign I have included some extra visualisations to consider where appropriate. As always you need to make these as bright and bold in your mind as possible, and there's no harm in adding some extra detail to each one. If you have your own ideas feel free to incorporate them too as you're far more likely to remember things you've come up with yourself.

Don't panic! You don't need to remember everything that follows straight away, so just browse through the descriptions and see how everything fits together as you read my thoughts on each sign.

**Top Tip:** *Feel free to change any of my choices to fictional characters you are more familiar with using the positive traits given for each sign. If you are feeling really brave you could always attempt to create an entirely new set of characters!*

### CAPRICORN - The Goat
JAM

### Atticus Finch

**Original visualisation: Imagine a goat with a white beard covered in JAM standing in a grassy field**

*Positive Traits: Serious, cold, disciplined, patient, focused, thoughtful, ambitious, indomitable, cautious, lucid, persistent, provident, steady, introverted, stern, wilful, hard-working, responsible, persevering, honest, realistic, loyal, reserved, resolute, moralistic, quiet, rigorous, attached and reliable.*

**Three possible careers**: Politician / Researcher / Jurist

**Character**: The lawyer Atticus Finch from 'To Kill A Mockingbird' - Atticus Finch perfectly sums up so much of the Capricorn personality as politician and researcher, but to be honest any well known fictional judge or politician is a good match for Capricorn - just look at those personality traits!

**NEW VISUALISATION: IMAGINE A GOAT WITH A WHITE BEARD COVERED IN JAM STANDING IN A GRASSY FIELD BEING CROSS-EXAMINED BY ATTICUS FINCH ABOUT THE JAM ROBBERY**

*Top Tip: If you're not that familiar with Atticus Finch it's easy to remember he's from 'To Kill A Mockingbird' as his surname is Finch, like the bird.*

# AQUARIUS - The Water Bearer
BREW

## Uhura

**Original visualisation: Imagine a beautiful princess pouring BEER through the air into a lake from a large vase**

*Positive Traits: Idealistic, altruistic, detached, independent, original, surprising, gifted, contradictory, innovative, humanistic, likable, friendly, self-confident, impassive, quiet, intuitive, creative, charitable, elusive, disconcerting, generous, tolerant, paradoxical, cannot stand any kind of constraint.*

**Three possible careers**: Astrologer / Astronaut / Actor

**Character**: The acting communications officer 'Uhura' from Star Trek - because she knows a lot about the stars (astrologer), she's also an astronaut along with everyone else on the starship Enterprise, and she's also in charge of communications (acting)

One of the reasons I have chosen Uhura from the crew of Star Trek is that she is a woman and Aquarius is very often depicted as a woman as in our original visualisation.

**NEW VISUALISATION: IMAGINE A BEAUTIFUL DARK SKINNED PRINCESS (UHURA) POURING BEER THROUGH THE AIR INTO A LAKE FROM A LARGE VASE**

*Top Tip: You can also imagine the space shuttle taking off in the background (astronaut), the lake could be at Cape Canaveral (astronaut) with millions of bright stars in the sky (astrologer) and a film crew could be filming it all (actor).*

## PISCES - The Fish
MARSH

## Captain Jack Sparrow

**Original visualisation: Imagine two playful fish swimming in a MARSH**

*Positive Traits: Emotional, sensitive, dedicated, adaptable, nice, wild, compassionate, romantic, imaginative, flexible, opportunist, intuitive, impossible to categorise, irrational, seductive, placid, secretive, introverted, pleasant, artistic, charming.*

**Three possible careers**: Traveller / Musician / Social Worker

**Character**: Captain Jack Sparrow from the 'Pirates Of The Caribbean' films - because he loves to travel the high seas, negotiates between the poor and the rich (well, between dead pirates and royalty, a form of social work!) and likes to sing the odd sea-shanty or two (musician)

I admit that Jack Sparrow's link with social work is rather tenuous but I'm sure his character would think that he was doing the poor and wretched a service. You can easily add one more career, 'jobs in remote places' without too much difficulty.

**NEW VISUALISATION: IMAGINE TWO PLAYFUL FISH SWIMMING IN A MARSH WHERE CAPTAIN JACK SPARROW HAS MOORED HIS BOAT**

*Top Tip: You can also imagine Jack Sparrow stepping from his boat onto an exotic island (travel) where he is welcomed by the local natives (social worker) while playing a sea shanty on a tin whistle (musician).*

## ARIES - The Ram
PILL

## Willy Wonka

**Original visualisation: Imagine an angry white ram with fiery eyes taking a PILL for his migraine**

*Positive Traits:* *Courageous, frank, enthusiastic, dynamic, fast, bold, expansive, warm, impulsive, adventurous, intrepid, warlike, competitive.*

**Three possible careers**: Entrepreneur / Businessman / Sportsman

**Character**: Willy Wonka from Willy Wonka And The Chocolate Factory - because he has grown his chocolate empire to be the largest in the kingdom (entrepreneur, businessman) and treats the whole thing as a game (sportsman)

I think there's something to be said for linking the idea of business as a big game for the character of Willy Wonka as I doubt he ever thought he'd done a days work in his life, similar to many entrepreneurs who see their work as a kind of sport. Most businessmen want to be the best, and most entrepreneurs want to be first. Sportsmen want both, and the Willy Wonka story starts with a game in the form of a golden ticket lottery.

**NEW VISUALISATION: IMAGINE AN ANGRY WHITE RAM WITH FIERY EYES BEING GIVEN A CHOCOLATE HEADACHE PILL BY WILLY WONKA**

*Top Tip:* *Why does the ram have a fiery eyes and a headache? Because he's been ramming into things!*

## TAURUS - The Bull
MAYONNAISE

### Chef

**Original visualisation: Imagine a strong headed bull in a fenced field licking MAYONNAISE out of a jar**

*Positive Traits: Faithful, constant, sturdy, patient, tough, persevering, strong, focused, sensual, stable, concrete, realistic, steady, loyal, robust, constructive, tenacious.*

**Three possible careers**: Cook / Artist / Singer

**Character**: Chef from 'South Park' - Chef is the cook from South Park, and is known for his musical outbursts (artist, singer)

Chef sums up a lot of the Taurus character traits. He's a faithful, loyal friend to the children but is somewhat static in his role as school chef. He's a strong and constant character that can always be relied upon to be constructive, whatever problems the children are facing.

**NEW VISUALISATION: IMAGINE A STRONG HEADED BULL IN A FENCED FIELD LICKING MAYONNAISE OUT OF A JAR HELD BY CHEF FROM SOUTH PARK**

## GEMINI - The Twins
TUNE

### John Keating

**Original visualisation: Imagine two identical young twins holding hands in the air whistling a TUNE together**

*Positive Traits: Expressive, lively, adaptable, quick-witted, humorous, sparkling, playful, sociable, clever, curious, whimsical, independent, polyvalent, brainy, flexible, ingenious, imaginative, charming, fanciful.*

**Three possible careers**: Teacher / Presenter / Salesman

**Character**: John Keating, the teacher from Dead Poet's Society (played by Robin Williams) - Although this fictional teacher only fits one of the possible careers for the Gemini exactly I can think of very few other fictional characters who sum up the Gemini's charm so well. A good teacher has to have presentation skills and has to sell his ideas to the class.

**NEW VISUALISATION: IMAGINE TWO IDENTICAL YOUNG TWINS HOLDING HANDS IN THE AIR WHISTLING A TUNE TO JOHN KEATING**

*Top Tip: If you find it hard to remember John Keating's name even though you can remember Robin Williams in the film, just remember that he's named after the famous English poet John Keats.*

## CANCER - The Crab
LIE

## Lovejoy

**Original visualisation: Imagine a big red crab on a sandy beach telling a LIE (crossed claws)**

*Positive Traits: Emotional, sentimental, peaceful, imaginative, sensitive, faithful, resistant, protective, vulnerable, generous, romantic, nostalgic, tender, poetic-minded, motherly or fatherly, dreamy, indolent, greedy, devoted.*

**Three possible careers**: The Hotel Trade / Property / Antique Dealer

**Character**: Lovejoy from the BBC TV series 'Lovejoy' - Lovejoy is primarily an antique dealer, but this leads him to spend quite some time in in stately homes (property) and guest houses (hotels). Antique shops, guest houses and stately homes are often a backdrop to such English middle class television series such as Lovejoy.

**NEW VISUALISATION: IMAGINE A BIG RED CRAB ON A SANDY BEACH TELLING A LIE TO LOVEJOY**

*Top Tip: What kind of lie? Well the crab is probably lying about his value, seeing as he's talking to an antique dealer! Big red crab - big red lie.*

## LEO - The Lion
GUST

## Yoda

**Original visualisation: Imagine a great lion with a fiery mane blown by a GUST of wind as it surveys its territory**

*Positive Traits:* *Proud, determined, strong-willed, loyal, solemn, generous, ambitious, courageous, heroic, conquering, creative, confident, seductive, happy, daring, fiery, majestic, honest, magnanimous, charismatic, responsible, noble, dramatic.*

**Three possible careers**: Spokesperson / Motivational Speaker / Leader

**Character**: Yoda the Jedi master from the Star Wars films - because he is the moral leader of the Jedi (spokesperson) and a motivator to Luke Skywalker and all other Jedi

It's hard to find a fictional character that is not only motivational but heroic in their own right. Yoda manages not only to train and lead but to be the moral compass of the Jedi as well.

**NEW VISUALISATION: IMAGINE A GREAT LION WITH A FIERY MANE BLOWN BY A GUST OF WIND AS IT SURVEYS ITS TERRITORY RIDDEN BY YODA**

*Top Tip:* *You can also imagine Yoda atop the lion addressing thousands of Star Wars creatures and races (spokesperson / motivational speaker / leader)*

# VIRGO - The Virgin
SCEPTER

# Miss Moneypenny

**Original visualisation: Imagine an innocent young girl in a flowery field holding a Scepter**

*Positive Traits: Brainy, perspicacious, attentive to detail and numbers, analytical, serious, competent, scrupulous, sensible, modest, logical, tidy, well organised, clean, hard-working, provident, honest, faithful, reserved, shy, helpful, a perfectionist.*

**Three possible careers**: Archivist / Executive Assistant / Secretary

**Character**: Miss Moneypenny from the Bond films - because she is secretary and assistant to M and although quiet, could well know more about the workings of the secret service than anyone else; how many secret documents could she have handled in her career? (archivist)

By virtue of being a Miss, there's a slim chance that Moneypenny could be a virgin which is enough to remind you of her innocent facade, even though she spends her life dealing with top secret information.

**NEW VISUALISATION: IMAGINE AN INNOCENT YOUNG GIRL (MISS MONEYPENNY) IN A FLOWERY FIELD HOLDING A SCEPTER**

# LIBRA - The Scales
OCTOPUS

## Edna Mode

**Original visualisation: Imagine an empty pair of scales weighing nothing but air held by an OCTOPUS**

*Positive Traits: Sentimental, charming, polite, refined, loyal, a pacifist, fair, distinguished, light-hearted, romantic, learned, ethereal, nice, well-groomed, a perfectionist, calm, sweet, tolerant, sociable, elegant, considerate, seductive, aesthetic, indulgent.*

**Three possible careers**: Fashionista / Artistic Creator / Beautician

**Character**: Fashionista Edna Mode from the Pixar film 'The Incredibles' - Edna is a cartoon fashionista who creates all the superheroes costumes in the film and strives to create beauty from the mundane.

Although Edna's character doesn't encompass the mediating skills of the Libra, she has everything else in abundance. Fortunately the traditional scales that represent Libra make it hard to forget the balancing and mediating aspect of the Libra.

**NEW VISUALISATION: IMAGINE AN EMPTY PAIR OF SCALES WEIGHING NOTHING BUT AIR HELD BY AN OCTOPUS HAVING A DRESS FITTING BY EDNA MODE**

*Top Tip: You can imagine Edna sizing up the octopus for a clothes fitting, perhaps 'Octopus Man' is a new superhero!*

### SCORPIO - The Scorpion
NO

### Sherlock Holmes

**Original visualisation: Imagine a scorpion scuttling about on the sand near an oasis with a NO entry sign**

*Positive Traits: Secretive, powerful, domineering, resistant, intuitive, asserted, charismatic, magnetic, strong-willed, perspicacious, passionate, creative, independent, vigorous, generous, loyal, hard-working, persevering, untamable, possessive, cunning, ambitious, sexual, proud, intense, competitive.*

**Three possible careers**: Psychiatrist / Detective / Police

**Character**: Sherlock Holmes - The London detective of 22b Baker Street, renowned for his intuition and deduction skills, understanding of the human psyche (psychiatrist) and close connections with the police.

**NEW VISUALISATION: IMAGINE A SCORPION SCUTTLING ABOUT ON THE SAND NEAR AN OASIS WITH A NO ENTRY SIGN BEING STALKED BY SHERLOCK HOLMES**

*Top Tip: Sherlock Holmes could be attempting to use his magnifying glass to burn the poor scorpion to death from the heat of the desert sun!*

# SAGITTARIUS - The Centaur
DISMEMBER

## Indiana Jones

**Original visualisation: Imagine a centaur with no legs (DISMEMBER) firing a flaming arrow from a bow**

*Positive Traits: Charismatic, fiery, energetic, likable, benevolent, tidy, jovial, optimistic, extraverted, amusing, straightforward, demonstrative, charming, independent, adventurous, straightforward, bold, exuberant, freedom-loving.*

**Three possible careers**: Explorer / Commercial Traveller / Philosopher

**Character**: Indiana Jones from the film 'Raiders Of The Lost Ark' - because a taste for adventure (explorer) with commercial gain (commercial traveller) typifies the character of Indiana Jones, but there is also a deeper side to him so enamoured with ancient culture (philosopher). He is also a pilot and an academic writer, two other professions associated with Sagittarius.

NEW VISUALISATION: IMAGINE A CENTAUR WITH NO LEGS FIRING A FLAMING ARROW FROM A BOW BEING RIDDEN BY INDIANA JONES

*Top Tip: You can imagine Indian Jones leading an expedition of tourists (explorer) into the desert on his herd of legless Centaurs (commercial traveller) as they go in search of the Philosopher's Stone (philosopher). You can even imagine the Centaurs looking like Sean Connery who appeared in the third Indiana Jones film! Pretty strange I'll admit, but hard to forget...*

# Visual Meanings

**Now you've had a chance to acquaint yourself with the twelve characters and the new combined visualisations it's time to commit them to memory**

Read through the following shortened list of the twelve star signs and characters with their expanded descriptions. Take the time to visualise each one of these as strongly as you can, building on the visualisations from the first half of this book. Spend at least ten seconds visualising each one. Close your eyes if you have to, and try to add as much colour and attention to detail as you can to each mental image.

**EXERCISE SIXTEEN - LEARNING - Two minutes, ten seconds each, repeat twice**

*Do this just in your head to start with!*

CAPRICORN - Imagine a goat with a white beard covered in jam standing in a grassy field being cross-examined by Atticus Finch about the jam robbery

AQUARIUS - Imagine a beautiful dark skinned princess (Uhura) pouring beer through the air into a lake from a large vase

PISCES - Imagine two playful fish swimming in a marsh where captain Jack Sparrow has moored his boat

ARIES - Imagine an angry white ram with fiery eyes being given a chocolate headache pill by Willy Wonka

TAURUS - Imagine a strong headed bull in a fenced field licking mayonnaise out of a jar held by Chef from south park

GEMINI - Imagine two identical young twins holding hands in the air whistling a tune to John Keating

CANCER - Imagine a big red crab on a sandy beach telling a lie to Lovejoy

LEO - Imagine a great lion with a fiery mane blown by a gust of wind ridden by Yoda as it surveys its territory

VIRGO - Imagine an innocent young girl (Miss Moneypenny) in a flowery field holding a scepter

LIBRA - Imagine an empty pair of scales weighing nothing but air held by an octopus having a dress fitting by Edna Mode

SCORPIO - Imagine a scorpion scuttling about on the sand near an oasis with a no entry sign being stalked by Sherlock Holmes

SAGITTARIUS - Imagine a centaur with no legs firing a flaming arrow from a bow being ridden by Indiana Jones

Now read through the above list out loud before you move on.

Let's see if we can recall a few of these new combined visualisations with just the literal description of each sign. I've mixed them up a bit so you're going to have to recall them at random.

## EXERCISE SEVENTEEN - RECALL - One minute, five seconds each

*When you recall each original visualisation the characters will hopefully come with them!*

I am The Scorpion. Explain my expanded mental image.
I am The Virgin. Explain my expanded mental image.
I am The Crab. Explain my expanded mental image.
I am The Bull. Explain my expanded mental image.
I am The Fish. Explain my expanded mental image.
I am The Goat. Explain my expanded mental image.
I am The Centaur. Explain my expanded mental image.

I am The Scales. Explain my expanded mental image.
We are The Twins. Explain my expanded mental image.
I am The Water Bearer. Explain my expanded mental image.
I am The Ram. Explain my expanded mental image.

How did you get on? You're probably able to remember most of each visualisation by now, but the question is whether the characters are sticking in your mind. Make a note of the signs and characters you're having the most problem remembering and spend a little more time visualising them.

If you're able to recall these signs with their characters more often than not, let's see how well you do at connecting the name of each sign with their mental image and character.

## EXERCISE EIGHTEEN - RECALL - One minute, five seconds each

*Now let's do it the other way around...*

What's the fictional character for Aries?
What's the fictional character for Aquarius?
What's the fictional character for Leo?
What's the fictional character for Libra?
What's the fictional character for Sagittarius?
What's the fictional character for Capricorn?
What's the fictional character for Pisces?
What's the fictional character for Taurus?
What's the fictional character for Cancer?
What's the fictional character for Virgo?
What's the fictional character for Scorpio?
What's the fictional character for Gemini?

If you're feeling quite confident in your mental ability to connect each star sign with their character, turn to the next chapter. If not, perhaps take a short break before reading through this chapter again.

# Cracking The Cusp

**The next three chapters deal exclusively with
The Cusp Zone**

We already know that people born before the 19th of the
month take the sign from the same month they were born in.

We also know that people born on or after the 23rd take the
sign from the next month.

The real problems arise when people are born in The Cusp
Zone between the 19th and the 23rd inclusive, where the start
dates for each sign tend to hop about.

In the next chapter, 'Twenty Twos Good News' you'll discover
that the second half of the year takes hardly no working out at
all, as the star signs between July and December all start on
the 23rd, apart from the last two, November and December
that start on the 22nd.

In the chapter 'Zodiac Phone Number' you'll learn a simple
sequence of 091-011 that will enable you to remember the
changing dates for the first half of the year.

And in the last chapter in this section, 'The Inner Cusp Zone'
you'll learn to shrink The Cusp Zone by two days so you've got
even less to worry about.

Although this is the most technical part of the book, if you
master these next three short chapters you'll never forget the
exact date of a star sign again.

# Cracking The Cusp 1 - Twenty Twos Good News

**Let's start working on being 100% accurate with dates for the SECOND half of the year**

One of the cool things about the 23rd Day Premise is that nearly ALL the months in the second half of the year from July to December have star signs that start on the 23rd. Only the last two months, November and December are one day different, starting on the 22nd.

This means that by using the 23rd Day Premise in the second half of the year you'll be right most of the time by default. All you've got to do is watch out for the last two months whose signs start on the 22nd.

Here are the star signs for the last six months of the year:

**Leo**: 23rd July to 22nd August

**Virgo**: 23rd August to 22nd September

**Libra**: 23rd September to 22nd October

**Scorpio**: 23rd October to 21st November

**Sagittarius**: 22nd November to 21st December

**Capricorn**: 22nd December to 22nd January

Don't worry about the actual signs for now. All you need to concern yourself with is the START DATE for each month. If you forget about the first digit of these months, we can think of them like the second part of a telephone number.

For instance, this:

23rd July
23rd August
23rd September
23rd October
22nd November
22nd December

Becomes this:

3
3
3
3
2
2

Which is this:

3333-22

This is a really simple pattern to remember, so when someone is born between July and December we can remember this to be 100% accurate.

**Example One:** Someone tells you they're born on the 22nd of November. They're in The Cusp Zone, and they're in the second half of the year. We know the pattern for start dates goes 3333-22 for the second half of the year, which means in November the next star sign starts on the 22nd. We've been told the 22nd of November, so the person's star sign starts in the next month, December. December, the dismembered Centaur, the person is a Sagittarius.

**Example Two:** Someone tells you they're born on the 22nd of August. They're in The Cusp Zone, and they're in the second half of the year. We know the pattern for start dates goes 3333-22 for the second half of the year, which means in

August the next star sign starts on the 23rd. We've been told the 22nd of August, so the person's star sign starts in the same month, August. August, the gust of wind blowing the Lion's mane, the person is a Leo.

Based on what you've learned so far, and using only dates from the second half of the year, try the next exercise. Initially this will take a bit more mental work but the same overall idea applies; use The 23rd Day Premise in the second half of the year unless someone's birthday is in November or December, when you use the 22nd instead.

## EXERCISE NINETEEN - RECALL - One minute, five seconds each

*What star sign are the following people?*

1. I was born on July 22nd.
2. I was born born on August 23rd.
3. I was born born on September 23rd.
4. I was born born on October 22nd.
5. I was born born on November 23rd.
6. I was born on December 22nd.
7 I was born born on November 21st.
8. I was born born on December 21st.
9. I was born born on August 22nd.
10. I was born born on September 22nd.

Make sure you are pretty happy with calculating star signs in the second half of the year before moving on to the next chapter, where we'll get on to working with the first half of the year too.

# Cracking The Cusp 2 - Zodiac Phone Number

**Now let's work on getting someone's star sign right 100% of the time by tackling the FIRST half of the year too**

We've already discussed the dates for the second half of the year but now we're going to look at the year as a whole.

Here is a list of all twelve star signs and their start dates, split into the first and second halves of the year. You can see that the start dates for the first half of the year are a lot more haphazard than the nice simple pattern of threes and twos that can be found in the second half of the year.

20th January - Aquarius
19th February - Pisces
21st March - Aries
20th April - Taurus
21st May - Taurus
21st June - Cancer
-
23rd July - Leo
23rd August - Virgo
23rd September - Libra
23rd October - Scorpio
22nd November - Sagittarius
22nd December - Capricorn

In the previous chapter we condensed the second half of the year into the sequence 3333-22. We can now do this with the first half of the year, which gives us the sequence 091-011.

Unfortunately, 091-011 isn't as easy to remember as 3333-22 but it's not exactly difficult. The nine doesn't mean the 29th of course, it actually means the 19th. As this is the only start day in the teens (all the others are twenty-something) it's not hard to remember that the 9 means 19th.

Putting this all together, we end up with what I call the Zodiac Phone Number: 091-011 3333-22. I remember the whole thing as 091-011, then all the threes, double two.

**Top Tip:** *The flash cards can be an enormous help when you're learning the Zodiac Phone Number!*

The threes and twos pattern in the second half of the year is so simple it's doubtful you'll ever forget it, leaving just the 091-011 to memorise. The first half of the year only contains zeros and ones (apart from the 9) making even this sequence relatively simple to remember. Of course the second half of the year only contains threes and twos.

In my own mind I tend to remember the Zodiac Phone Number like this:

0 January
9 February
1 March
0 April
1 May
1 June
-
3 July
3 August
3 September
3 October
2 November
2 December


Whenever I have to calculate someone's star sign I look down this list in my mind's eye as I tend to remember it more like a shape than a sequence. Of course you can remember it however you like, and the more you test yourself the more you will recall and remember. To be honest I hardly worry about the second half of the year as it's so simple to remember.

*Top Tip: If you have a problem remembering where the year splits into two, just remember it's between the two Js, June and July.*

Here's an exercise based solely on the numbers of the months. Use the Zodiac Phone Number to help you!

## EXERCISE TWENTY - RECALL - One minute, five seconds each

*For these six questions just remember the sequence 091-011*

### January - June

1. What day does the 5th month's star sign start on?
2. What day does the 2nd month's star sign start on?
3. What day does the 6th month's star sign start on?
4. What day does the 1st month's star sign start on?
5. What day does the 3rd month's star sign start on?
6. What day does the 4th month's star sign start on?

*For these six questions it's easy to recall the sequence 3333-22*

### July - December
7. What day does the 12th month's star sign start on?
8. What day does the 7th month's star sign start on?
9. What day does the 9th month's star sign start on?
10. What day does the 11th month's star sign start on?
11. What day does the 10th month's star sign start on?
12. What day does the 8th month's star sign start on?

You're probably finding the second half of the year a lot easier to remember than the first half of the year. Here are some extra tips in case you're still a bit fingers and thumbs:

* January, February and March are months 1, 2 and 3. We should never have to calculate those. They correspond with 0-9-1.

* All dates in the second half of the year end in a 3, apart from the last two that end in a 2. They don't really need calculating either.

* That leaves us with April, May and June which correspond with 0-1-1 in the zodiac phone number. These are probably the only months that you're going to have problems with. If you can remember that April is the 4th month you've got a head start.

**Top Tip:** *Think of April FOOL and you'll remember that April is the FOURTH month.*

With this in mind, let's see how you do with this next exercise where you're going to have to convert the month to a number first, before knowing the start date of each sign.

## EXERCISE TWENTY ONE - RECALL - One minute, five seconds each

*What date does the star sign that begins in each of these months start?*

1. May
2. February
3. June
4. January
5. March
6. April
7. December
8. July

9. September
10. November
11. October
12. August

Don't forget that this sequence is shown on each flash card and this can quickly help you get up to speed when you're learning and practicing. By this point in the book you should really be using the audio to help get this information into your head too.

# 9. VIRGO The Virgin
## September – SCEPTER

Imagine an innocent young girl in a flowery field holding a SCEPTER

*August 23rd - September 22nd*                    MISS MONEYPENNY

| 1 | 2 | 3 | 4 | 5 | 6 | 7 | 8 | 9 | 10 | 11 | 12 |
|---|---|---|---|---|---|---|---|---|----|----|----|
| JAN | FEB | MAR | APR | MAY | JUN | JLY | AUG | SEP | OCT | NOV | DEC |
| 0 | 9 | 1 | 0 | 1 | 1 | 3 | 3 | 3 | 3 | 2 | 2 |
| | | | | | | | | Libra | | | |

*Don't forget to download the flash cards and audio
to help you learn the system as quickly as possible!*

# Cracking The Cusp #3 - The Inner Cusp Zone

**A final nugget of time-saving advice before we put everything together**

As we have discussed, The Cusp Zone ranges from the 19th to the 23rd of each month, but in practice you don't need to use all five days in your calculations. In fact, you can ignore the outer dates and only use the Inner Cusp Zone.

## INNER CUSP ZONE 20th - 22nd

The Inner Cusp Zone is the 20th to the 22nd inclusive and helps us simplify our calculations a great deal:

*Someone born BEFORE the 20th takes the sign from the same month UNLESS its the 19th of February (the only 19th that a star sign starts)*

*Someone born AFTER the 22nd takes the star sign from the next month*

So The Inner Cusp Zone isn't really a new calculation. It actually stops us having to calculate so much:

*Treat every 19th as if it was in the sign from the same month UNLESS it's the 19th of February*

*Only think of dates as being outside the 20th and 22nd of the month when deciding whether you're in The Cusp Zone or not*

**Example One:** You are told someone is born on the 19th October. Their birthday falls before The Inner Cusp Zone, but it's a 19th; however it's not the 19th of February, so they take the sign from the month they were born in. October, Octopus, Libra.

**Example Two:** You are told someone is born on the [ ]
February. And February has the ONLY 19th where yo[u]
the star sign from the next month, March. March, Ma[ ]
Pisces. (February 19th is ALWAYS a Pisces of cours[e]

**Example Three:** You are told someone is born on the 23rd of
June. Their birthday falls AFTER the inner cusp zone, so their
star sign comes from the next month, July. July, Lying, Cancer.

Of course, when someone's birthday falls inside The Inner
Cusp Zone you use the Zodiac Phone Number as per usual.

*Top Tip: 19th of February is always a Pisces. If you're going
to bother remembering one date for one sign, make it that
one.*

So, using the inner cusp zone stops you thinking so much
about all those twenty-threes in the second half of the year,
and allows you to forget about nineteens UNLESS it's actually
the 19th of February.

Now let's do an exercise to see if you know which star sign
each of these next birthdays take.

**EXERCISE TWENTY TWO - RECALL - One minute, five
seconds each**

*Don't forget, all 19th dates take the star sign from the month
they are in, apart from the 19th February which takes the next
one!*

1. 19th May
2. 19th January
3. 19th April
4. 19th June
5. 19th December
6. 19th February
7. 19th October
8. 19th July

. 19th March
10. 19th August
11. 19th September
12. 19th November

In this next exercise, only worry if a date is outside The Inner Cusp Zone, before the 20th / after the 22nd.

## EXERCISE TWENTY THREE - RECALL - One minute, five seconds each

*How quickly can you figure out each sign?*

1. 19th February
2. 20th November
3. 23rd August
4. 19th September
5. 19th May
6. 20th January
7. 21st April
8. 20th October
9. 21st July
10. 22nd March
11. 22nd June
12. 23rd December

Hopefully by doing these exercises you can see how much easier it is to only worry about birthdays that are on the 20th, 21st and 22nd, treating all other dates as before or after the Inner Cusp Zone.

*This is the end of the 'Cracking The Cusp' section. You may need to run through it a few times, but don't be too hard on yourself as it takes a little while to sink in. All it takes is practice and don't forget; even if you're off by one you're probably doing way better than most people and can be forgiven for just missing a star sign when you're just starting out!*

# Exposition

**Knowing the character for each star sign is one thing, but you need to practice talking about them**

It's really useful to be able to connect a relevant fictional character to each star sign, but that alone is not enough; we need to use these characters as a way of remembering each sign's preferred professions, and ultimately each sign's character traits. We need to work backwards from each character by forming a string of logical conclusions in our minds, and the best way to practice doing this is by talking out loud as if we were telling someone about themselves.

If you've read my book 'The James Bond Cold Reading' you will know that I'm a big fan of 'talking the talk' and I believe that unless you can relate your ideas to someone in an interesting way then there's little point in learning this stuff in the first place. Talking out loud puts you on the spot and forces you to think, and the more you practice putting thoughts into spoken words the quicker you'll learn how to express the ideas behind each sign. Talking to an empty room is a great way to practice but only by striking up conversations with other people will you expand your knowledge and add multiple layers to what you've already learned here. This book can give you a framework but you need to build on it with real world experience by listening to people and how they relate to their own star signs as much as you can.

Let's take another look at what I came up with in a previous section about Sherlock Holmes, who is Scorpio's character:

He is certainly cunning. He has an amazing ability to work things out and to see 'what's what'. He is incredibly intuitive and doesn't miss a thing. This can make him seem quite insular at times but he's not being rude - he's thinking. He never gives up and sees things through to their logical conclusion. This can make him appear quite cold but in fact

71

he's quite a romantic character and is prone to acts of spontaneity (such as picking up his violin and playing it while he thinks!) He's competitive and loves a challenge, and is rarely proven wrong. He uses his quite considerable charm to get what he wants but this never feels forced, although sometimes it can come across as arrogant. He can be a very loyal friend (as he was to Dr Watson) but would prefer to have the upper hand in a relationship as he is somewhat independent in mind as well as action. He works hard and plays hard and doesn't see much of a distinction between the two. People are drawn to him but as he is quite a complex character; some people may feel that they've never really got to know him, even if they've been friends for years.

Talking about Sherlock Holmes is all very interesting, but if I was to meet a person called Lauren who told me they were a Scorpio I could say something similar to the above but related directly to them:

*"So Lauren, you're a Scorpio, and Scorpios can be cunning. Scorpios have an amazing ability to work things out and to see 'what's what', they're intuitive and don't miss a thing. This can make them seem quite insular at times but they're not being rude - they're thinking. Scorpios never give up and see things through to their logical conclusion. I think you might appear cold but in fact you're quite romantic and have your spontaneous moments. You're quite competitive and Scorpios love a challenge, are you proven wrong that often? Scorpios can be quite charming but some people think you're a bit arrogant. You can be a very loyal friend but prefer to have the upper hand as you're somewhat independent in mind as well as action. Scorpios work hard and play hard and although some people are drawn to you you're quite a complex character and some people may feel that they've never really got to know you."*

Even though I'm using the concept of Sherlock Holmes as a springboard for my explanation of the Scorpio personality, I'm also using it to remind me of the Scorpio's preferred professions as I attempt to describe Lauren to herself. Lauren will have no idea I'm thinking about Sherlock Holmes at all. Once I find out she's a Scorpio I immediately see Scorpio The Scorpion being stalked by Sherlock Holmes in my mind's eye and I can start a conversation immediately, explaining the Scorpion personality via Sherlock Holmes without even mentioning the famous detective once. I'll sound like I know what I'm talking about and all I'm doing is describing a character I'm already quite familiar with.

**Top Tip:** *Don't describe what the characters DO, describe what they're LIKE.*

In the next section are some very short examples of what you could say for each sign based on their characters. Read through them once or twice if you wish, but don't go learning these by heart; they're only for reference and you should only look to them when you're in need of a little inspiration.

# Character Exposition

**A few short examples of what you might say about each star sign based on their character, preferred professions and traits**

Here are some examples I've created myself by simply running with the idea of each star sign's character. These are only for reference and should not be learned, but show what you can do when you just run with the ideas for each fictional character.

**CAPRICORN - Atticus Finch from 'To Kill A Mockingbird'**
Politician / Researcher / Jurist

Positive Traits: Serious, cold, disciplined, patient, focused, thoughtful, ambitious, indomitable, cautious, lucid, persistent, provident, steady, introverted, stern, wilful, hard-working, responsible, persevering, honest, realistic, loyal, reserved, resolute, moralistic, quiet, rigorous, attached and reliable.

*"You're a Capricorn, and you can be very thorough when you want to be. Patient and focused yet ambitious, you are able to tackle jobs that many other people find tiresome or just downright confusing. This can make you appear somewhat introverted but you just need to get things right in your mind before you decide on your path of action. Ever the diplomat, your hard-working and realistic manner make you a natural leader where clarity is required, the only downside to this being that you can appear a little cold at times. However you are generous with your time and your persistence often pays off doing good for others. You leave no stone unturned and can be quite a formidable opponent when challenged as you often seem one step ahead of the crowd and have all the facts at your fingertips."*

## AQUARIUS - Communications Officer Uhura from 'Star Trek'

Astrologer / Astronaut / Actor

Positive Traits: Idealistic, altruistic, detached, independent, original, surprising, gifted, contradictory, innovative, humanistic, likable, friendly, self-confident, impassive, quiet, intuitive, creative, charitable, elusive, disconcerting, generous, tolerant, paradoxical, cannot stand any kind of constraint.

*"You're an Aquarius, and Aquarians are known for their ability to communicate and get things across. You are also good at working in a team, but you do need to be left on your own sometimes to just get on with things. You don't have a problem being the centre of attention and you like an audience when you're in the mood. Aquarians find life and the universe quite fascinating and like exploring new ideas, although they prefer to share the experience with other people. You can find yourself looking at the stars sometimes wondering what it's all about, but you're fairly grounded as a person. Aquarians like connecting with others so I wouldn't be surprised if you thought about people as much as you did about life, the universe and everything; you're also interested in knowing how people tick."*

## PISCES - Captain Jack Sparrow from 'Pirates Of The Caribbean'

Traveller / Musician / Social Worker

Positive Traits: Emotional, sensitive, dedicated, adaptable, nice, wild, compassionate, romantic, imaginative, flexible, opportunist, intuitive, impossible to categorise, irrational, seductive, placid, secretive, introverted, pleasant, artistic, charming.

*"Pisces are well known for their ability to bring people together and are always there when you need someone to talk to. You'd probably like to travel more as you like seeing new places and meeting new people, and you have a creative*

75

streak that is either musical or you're a big fan of music. You tend to take the side of the underdog and occasionally bite off more than you can chew which can get you into trouble. Pisces people are a lot more romantic than people give them credit for but on occasion they can be somewhat impulsive. Luckily you can probably get away with murder as you have your fair share of charm that you can turn on when you see fit. You enjoy helping others and some people don't know the lengths you go to to keep everyone happy."

## ARIES - Willy Wonka from 'Willy Wonka And The Chocolate Factory'
Entrepreneur / Businessman / Sportsman

Positive Traits: Courageous, frank, enthusiastic, dynamic, fast, bold, expansive, warm, impulsive, adventurous, intrepid, warlike, competitive.

"The entrepreneurial spirit of Aries is well known. Aries love being involved and coming up with new things and you have a certain competitiveness about you. You can show this in strange ways though and some people may think you're slightly eccentric. In the past you've probably felt a bit detached from everything while you're doing your own thing, but you've always had this need to have other people around you, as long as you're in charge that is! Aries can be quite shrewd and when they decide what they want they can be hard to stop. You do have a controlling side that you have to be careful of but you like to have fun and you can be pretty playful at times when you need to lose some steam and let your guard down. After all, it can be pretty hard keeping it up!"

## TAURUS - Chef from 'South Park'
Cook / Artist / Singer

Positive Traits: Faithful, constant, sturdy, patient, tough, persevering, strong, focused, sensual, stable, concrete, realistic, steady, loyal, robust, constructive, tenacious.

*"Everybody knows that Taurus is the bull, and sometimes this can be misinterpreted as a stick in the mud. It's not true! You are usually there for everybody in times of need and that's more than can be said for most people. You can also be pretty creative in the kitchen and if any star sign is going to sing in the shower it's going to be Taurus. I'm not sure what you do but Taureans can also be pretty good at drawing or painting too although they can get a bit carried away and don't always have the best taste! People can often turn to you for advice and you're not afraid to give it or to speak your mind either, although some of the time you feel like your advice is falling on deaf ears. You're quite resilient however so you're able to pick yourself up time and time again."*

## GEMINI - John Keating from 'Dead Poets Society'
Teacher / Presenter / Salesman

Positive Traits: Expressive, lively, adaptable, quick-witted, humorous, sparkling, playful, sociable, clever, curious, whimsical, independent, polyvalent, brainy, flexible, ingenious, imaginative, charming, fanciful.

*"You're a Gemini, and Gemini's can be showoffs, but not in the way most people think. Gemini's are really good at explaining things and sometimes you like being the centre of attention but not in a 'look at me' kind of way, more like a teacher. You're pretty good at getting your own way when you want it, and you could probably sell ice to eskimos if you had to. You are really enthusiastic about whatever it is you're doing and this enthusiasm can be infectious, you know how to have fun even when you're working! You care passionately about what you believe in and you aren't scared to explain your opinion to*

others, although you have to be careful as some people aren't as clever as you and can get the wrong end of the stick."

## CANCER - Lovejoy from the BBC TV series 'Lovejoy'
The Hotel Trade / Property / Antique Dealer

Positive Traits: Emotional, sentimental, peaceful, imaginative, sensitive, faithful, resistant, protective, vulnerable, generous, romantic, nostalgic, tender, poetic-minded, motherly or fatherly, dreamy, indolent, greedy, devoted.

*"You've got a good eye for a bargain like most Cancers, and although you may not know as much about history as you'd like you certainly find it fascinating. You like a bit of drama and some people might think you're slightly nosey, when in fact you're just interested in other people. Your have a sense of style of your own which is reflected in your home surroundings, but you might also enjoy architecture although your tastes might be somewhat conservative. You like to be wined and dined on occasion and there's a chance than even though you like staying in nice hotels when you have the chance, the thought might have crossed your mind to own or run one in the future. Quite a few Cancers work in property and I wouldn't be surprised if you've moved house quite often."*

## LEO - Yoda from 'Star Wars'
Spokesperson / Motivational Speaker / Leader

Positive Traits: Proud, determined, strong-willed, loyal, solemn, generous, ambitious, courageous, heroic, conquering, creative, confident, seductive, happy, daring, fiery, majestic, honest, magnanimous, charismatic, responsible, noble, dramatic.

*"Whether people know it or not you can be quite a force to reckon with. Leos have a lot of leadership skills, but leadership comes in so many forms it can be hard for some to see. There are those who motivate others by quietly sitting in the background giving advice from a distance, and others who*

*take the reigns, willing to risk life and limb on the front lines. You probably try to strike a happy balance. Even if you don't feel that confident about speaking in public you'd be pretty good at it, as you have quite a lot of life experience to draw upon. Sometimes it may not feel natural, but you might find yourself in a position when you have to speak up for others who are less able to stand up for themselves. You don't run into things hastily however and choose your moments wisely."*

## VIRGO - Miss Moneypenny from the Bond films
Archivist / Executive Assistant / Secretary

Positive Traits: Brainy, perspicacious, attentive to detail and numbers, analytical, serious, competent, scrupulous, sensible, modest, logical, tidy, well-organised, clean, hard-working, provident, honest, faithful, reserved, shy, helpful, a perfectionist.

*"You can be both hopelessly romantic yet incredibly astute and calm, one of the idiosyncrasies of being a Virgo. Virgo's can be incredibly precise when they want to be and your version of perfection might seem very different to others around you. The problem with this is you can often find yourself picking up the pieces that other people have left behind, but this doesn't seem to bother you as you're very good at remembering what's happened and you can be a stickler for the finer details. You can easily tell what people are best at and help them with their shortcomings for their own good. You have a certain amount of charm however and even though you can be diligent and get on with what is necessary there's a lot more to you than meets the eye and you always know more than you are willing to tell."*

## LIBRA - Edna Mode from 'The Incredibles'
Fashionista / Artistic Creator / Beautician

Positive Traits: Sentimental, charming, polite, refined, loyal, a pacifist, fair, distinguished, light-hearted, romantic, learned, ethereal, nice, well-groomed, a perfectionist, calm, sweet, tolerant, sociable, elegant, considerate, seductive, aesthetic, indulgent.

*"Libras are well known for their sense of balance in all things, but what is overlooked is how much of this is creative balance. You know what you like and you're not scared to share that vision with the rest of the world. Sometimes this can show itself in the clothes you wear, but not always; some Libras can be happily scruffy while they paint a masterpiece. You don't do 'ugly' and you have a knack for turning things on their head for the best and you can see the good in almost everything. Some people think you're shallow but in actual fact you sense things on a deeper level than most and can be quite instinctual. You're not necessarily a show off as you like sharing what you're doing with everyone and self expression comes very naturally to you. Just don't become too superficial."*

## SCORPIO - Sherlock Holmes from the books by Sir Arthur Conan Doyle
Psychiatrist / Detective / Police

Positive Traits: Secretive, powerful, domineering, resistant, intuitive, asserted, charismatic, magnetic, strong-willed, perspicacious, passionate, creative, independent, vigorous, generous, loyal, hard-working, persevering, untamable, possessive, cunning, ambitious, sexual, proud, intense, competitive.

*"You're a Scorpio, and Scorpios can be cunning. Scorpios have an amazing ability to work things out and to see 'what's what', they're intuitive and don't miss a thing. This can make them seem quite insular at times but they're not being rude - they're thinking. Scorpios never give up and see things*

*through to their logical conclusion. I think you might appear cold but in fact you're quite romantic and have your spontaneous moments. You're quite competitive and Scorpios love a challenge, are you proven wrong that often? Scorpios can be quite charming but some people think you're a bit arrogant. You can be a very loyal friend but prefer to have the upper hand as you're somewhat independent in mind as well as action. Scorpios work hard and play hard and although some people are drawn to you you're quite a complex character and some people may feel that they've never really got to know you."*

## SAGITTARIUS - Indiana Jones from 'Raiders Of The Lost Ark'
Explorer / Commercial Traveller / Philosopher

Positive Traits: Charismatic, fiery, energetic, likable, benevolent, tidy, jovial, optimistic, extraverted, amusing, demonstrative, charming, independent, adventurous, straightforward, bold, exuberant, freedom-loving.

*"You're a Sagittarius, and like most Sagittarians you have quite an adventurous streak. You have a strong need for personal freedom not only in the world but in your mind, although you can tend to dwell and over-think things a little. You are likable and fun-loving and have a lot of energy yet you can also be very down to earth and practical; you can get things done and usually get others to help you. You can be fiercely independent at times yet you are quite often there for the more needy. As you tend to be pretty good at logistics you can usually work things out for yourself and other people; you can often find yourself put in charge, even though you don't always feel that comfortable in the driving seat when there are others involved. In that sense you are more like a lone adventurer and find it easier to think and do things when you're alone, even though you do need people around you to help you see things through."*

81

# Recap

**Let's recap what we have learned so far**

1. We have created a visual image for each month of the year

2. We have visualised a unique mental image for each star sign

3. We have combined each month image with each star sign image to become one visualisation

4. We have learnt that each star sign lasts roughly a month and starts between the 19th and 23rd of each month, called The Cusp Zone

5. We have learnt how to calculate a star sign from any given date with 87% accuracy by using The 23rd Day Premise

6. We have learnt how to assign a fictional character to each star sign, based on each sign's traits and preferred professions

7. We have combined these fictional characters with our previous visualisations

8. We have learnt how the second half of the year's star signs all start on the 23rd, apart from the last two that start on the 22nd by using the pattern 3333-22

9. We have learnt the Zodiac Phone Number that also includes the first half of the year with the pattern 091-011

10. We have learnt to use The Inner Cusp Zone to calculate outside the 20th to 22nd of the month and to watch out for the 19th of February

# The Three Steps

**From hearing a person's date of birth to telling them their star sign in three steps**

Most people's birthdays fall out of the Inner Cusp Zone and only one in 365 people will have a birthday on the 19th of February, so most of the time you're only one simple calculation away from telling someone about their star sign.

With a bit of practice you'll be reeling off signs as if you've known them all your life; as soon as you arrive at April you'll see Willy Wonka feeding a chocolate pill to Aries The Ram, the moment you arrive at September you'll see Miss Moneypenny as Virgo The Virgin holding a scepter.

Of course you're going to need to practice all of this until it's second nature, and if you've got this far by cheating and not doing the exercises you're going to need to go back and work your way through the book properly. It may seem long winded but I assure you it's not; you'll be amazed how quickly you can remember all this stuff as it's hardly technical at all.

Should there be any doubt in your mind as to how the system works in practice, here are The Three Steps. Run through it a few times with some imaginary dates to see how it comes together. Most of the time you'll never get past Step Two!

# The Three Steps Sequence

**Step One: Is the person's birthday on the 19th?**

*If not, go to the next step...*

**If it is:**

> If their birthday is February 19th their sign belongs to the next month, March. Remember their sign. (Always Pisces!)

> If their birthday is ANY OTHER 19th then their sign starts in the named month. Remember their sign.

**Step Two: Is the person's birthday OUTSIDE The Inner Cusp Zone? (Before the 20th / After the 22nd)**

*If it's not, go to the next step...*

**If it is:**

> If it's before, their star sign belongs to the month they named. Stay with the month and remember their sign.

> If it's after, their star sign belongs to the next month. Move a month ahead and remember their sign.

**Step Three: We're in The Inner Cusp Zone! (20th to 22nd inclusive)**

*Use the Zodiac Phone Number 091-011 (3333)-22*

> If the person's birthday is before the start date for that month, their star sign comes from the same month. Remember their sign.

> If the person's birthday is on or after the start date for that month, their star sign belongs to the next month. <u>Remember their sign</u>.

**THAT'S IT!**

Of course, once you've remembered their sign you can do what you like with it. You could just make a note of it so you know more about them. Or you could tell them all about their star sign and how much (or not) they're similar to it. It's entirely up to you.

The moment you remember their sign you'll know their sign's fictional character and you can use this information how you like.

# Compatibility

## Which star signs get along?

People often use star signs to measure compatibility between one another. Each sign has an element connected with them and these elements have different traits. The elements are already incorporated into the descriptions of each and every sign in this book, so you already know them!

Take a read through the four elements and think about the visualisation for each sign. Can you see the connection?

### + Fire Signs: Aries / Leo / Sagittarius

*A fiery person with an enthusiasm and drive to express himself*

### + Air Signs: Gemini / Libra / Aquarius

*An airy, conceptual thinker with excellent social and communicative skills*

### - Earth Signs: Taurus / Virgo / Capricorn

*An earthy, practical character who very much lives in the real world*

### - Water Signs: Cancer / Scorpio / Pisces

*The phrase 'Still waters run deep' is true for the water signs as they are emotional, empathic and sensitive*

As you can see, each of the elements is fairly self-explanatory. The Fire and Air signs are self expressive (+) and the Earth and Water signs are more down to earth and self contained (-). These groupings are called 'polarities'.

Let's look at the star sign descriptions again as they've appeared throughout this book. I've highlighted the relevant sections, and omitted the twelve fictional characters for clarity.

**Fire Signs: Aries / Leo / Sagittarius**

*The idea of fire has been hidden in the descriptions of Aries, Leo and Sagittarius*

ARIES - The Ram - Imagine an angry white ram with **fiery eyes** and curly horns
LEO - The Lion - Imagine a great lion with a **fiery mane** surveying its territory
SAGITTARIUS - The Centaur - Imagine a centaur firing a **flaming arrow** from a bow

**Air Signs: Gemini / Libra / Aquarius**

*The idea of air has been hidden in the descriptions of Gemini, Libra and Aquarius*

GEMINI - The Twins - Imagine two identical young twins holding hands **in the air**
LIBRA - The Scales - Imagine an empty pair of scales **weighing nothing but air**
AQUARIUS - The Water Bearer - Imagine a beautiful princess pouring water **through the air** into a lake from a vase

**Earth Signs: Taurus / Virgo / Capricorn**

*All the earth signs are standing in a field*

TAURUS - The Bull - Imagine a strong headed bull in a **fenced field**
VIRGO - The Virgin - Imagine an innocent young girl in a **flowery field**
CAPRICORN - The Goat - Imagine a goat with a white beard standing in a **grassy field**

**Water Signs: Cancer / Scorpio / Pisces**

*The water signs are all either on the sand or in the water anyway!*

CANCER - The Crab - Imagine a big red crab on a **sandy beach**
SCORPIO - The Scorpion - Imagine a scorpion scuttling about on the sand **near an oasis**
PISCES - The Fish - Imagine two playful fish swimming **in the sea**

If you've worked through this book diligently then you need only remember a visualisation to see which element is attached to any star sign you may think of. The moment you think of Sagittarius and his fiery arrow you immediately know that Sagittarius is a Fire sign, for instance.

If you've previously not taken too much notice of these ideas then it won't take you too long to go back and just have a quick re-visualisation of each one, making sure to emphasise these elements the second time round!

*Top Tip: There are only a couple of things that could mix you up here. The first one is that Aquarius, although being a water bearer, is actually an AIR sign, hence the description 'pouring water through the air'. The other is that Scorpio is actually a water sign, even though scorpions are usually associated with deserts. You can remember this if you just think of this silly joke - Q: Why isn't Aquarius a water sign? A: Because she jumped into the air when Scorpio stung her (and Scorpio took her place as a water sign).*

It's one thing to know the elements connected with each star sign, but you need to understand how they work together. Apart from remembering the obvious idea that people with the same star signs tend to get along, there are a few other things to remember:

**People get along well with people of their own element**
*Air people get on with other Air people*
*Fire people get on with other Fire people*
*Earth people get on with other Earth people*
*Water people get on with other Water people*

**People with different elements from the same polarity CLASH**
*Fire people don't get on too well with Air people*
*Earth people don't get on too well with Water people*

**Example One:** Geoff is a Capricorn. He quite likes Mary who is a Taurus. Will they get on? If we remember Capricorn the goat standing in a grassy field, and Taurus the bull in a fenced field they are both in fields, making both of them EARTH. People get on well with people of their own element, so Geoff and Mary look like a good match.

**Example Two:** Sarah is an Aries. Sarah quite likes Rob who is a Gemini. Will they get on? If we remember Aries the ram with his fiery eyes, and the Gemini twins holding hands in the air, we know that Aries is a FIRE sign and Gemini is an AIR sign. Sarah and Rob are the same polarity (+) but different elements (Fire and Air) so there's a chance they won't hit it off.

If you find yourself talking to someone about their compatibility with someone else you'll find that using the characters associated with each star sign can also give you a lot of food for thought. For instance, Geoff and Mary are represented by Atticus Finch (Capricorn) and Chef from South Park (Taurus). Of course the idea of Atticus Finch and Chef getting together is somewhat fantastical (but still quite good fun) but the idea of a lawyer and researcher type getting together with a solid and dependable chef type sounds promising. Likewise the idea of Sarah and Rob are represented by Aries (Willy Wonka) and John Keating (Gemini). There's a chance the entrepreneurial businesswoman in Sarah won't really get along with the charming teacher and flights of fancy of Rob. Although perhaps his salesmanship is the feature that she finds so appealing?

As you can see, letting yourself think about relationships between the signs in this way is great fun, and the added dimension of using fictional characters to describe each sign lets your imagination go off on all kinds of tangents.

## EXERCISE TWENTY FIVE

*What could you say about each of these couples?*

1. Sagittarius and Aquarius
2. Taurus and Cancer
3. Gemini and Virgo
4. Scorpio and Leo
5. Capricorn and Libra

What could you say about the dynamics of each of these groups of people?

6. Gemini, Libra and Aquarius
7. Aries, Virgo and Capricorn
8. Scorpio, Taurus and Leo
9. Cancer, Capricorn and Gemini
10. Gemini, Taurus and Sagittarius

Take the time to think about these questions as it's really useful to think about how the various signs connect with each other on a day to day basis.

# The Real Zodiac Year

Although I've based my system on the normal course of a year from January through December, the zodiac year actually starts with Aries and ends with Pisces, from April through March (so strictly speaking the zodiac year starts on 21st March).

You can see some of this history reflected in the actual names of the months as they stand today:

**September** has the sound SEPT as in seven, and is the seventh month in the zodiac, even though it's the ninth month of the year.

**October** with the sound Oct as in eight, which we see in words like 'octave', is the eighth month in the zodiac, even though it's the tenth month of the year.

**November** as in NINE is the ninth month in the zodiac, even though it's the eleventh month of the year.

**December** as in DEC as in decimal is the tenth sign of the zodiac, even though it's the twelfth month of the year.

Just something to bear in mind for when you get into a discussion about zodiac signs or if you read further into the subject.

# Leap Years

Every once in a while you're going to meet someone who was born during a leap year on the 29th of February. Of course as their star sign starts right at the end of the month they take the star sign from the next month of March, making them a Pisces.

# Character List

**A quick rundown of all the characters I've chosen
for this book**

In case there are any characters I've mentioned in this book
that you're unfamiliar with, here is a brief summary for each of
them. In my quest to make this book as accessible as possible
I've opted for characters from popular rather than literary
culture where possible. If you've never seen 'Dead Poets
Society' or 'The Incredibles' then I urge you to do so. They're
both very films good for entirely different reasons, and of
course 'To Kill A Mockingbird' is a literary classic as well as a
must-see movie.

### Communications Officer Uhura from 'Star Trek'

According to Star Trek's futuristic storyline, Uhura is from the
United States Of Africa and speaks Swahili. Although she was
played by Nichelle Nichols in the original television series her
role has been continued in the 2009 film reboot of the Star
Trek franchise, casting a younger Uhura in a parallel universe
played by Zoe Saldana.

### Captain Jack Sparrow from 'Pirates Of The Caribbean'

One of Johnny Depp's most memorable roles, the camp and
previously alive Jack Sparrow has been swashbuckling his
way through each  of the 'Pirates' films with varying degrees of
success. Part villain, part lovable rogue, completely dead, he's
marauded distant shores on both sides of the afterlife as well
as having had his fair share of booty on the high seas.

### Willy Wonka from 'Willy Wonka And The Chocolate Factory'

Played brilliantly by Gene Wilder in this timeless classic, Willy
Wonka's eccentricity appears harsh at first as he dispatches

greedy and selfish children at every turn. However, by the end of the film you can't help but love him and his warped sense of humor and childlike naivety; by the credits you're wishing you could go up in a Great Glass Elevator too. Of course we have the author Roald Dahl's brilliant mind to thank for inventing it all and the book is essential reading for children.

## Chef from 'South Park'

Featuring the voice of soul singer Isaac Hayes, Chef is one of the only characters in South Park that the kids can turn to for moral guidance. Seeing himself as a ladies man, Chef has a tendency to go off on sensual musical interludes, often singing songs that are way over the children's heads with little to do with the matter at hand. Unfortunately Chef had to be killed off when Hayes quit the show as he disagreed with the lampooning of Scientology, of which he is a follower.

## John Keating from 'Dead Poets Society'

People as charismatic as John Keating can teach anything to anybody and this was one of Robin Williams' more restrained performances. Mr Keating manages to bring literature to life with his unorthodox yet creative teaching methods and inspires the class to take notice of the classics for the first time. It goes horribly wrong and he gets the sack, and we get to lament the fact that none of us ever had a teacher that good.

## Lovejoy from the BBC TV series 'Lovejoy'

If there's a character that I've chosen that you probably haven't heard of it's this one. Quintessentially English and shown primarily on the BBC, Lovejoy told the story of a cheeky yet charming antiques dealer who roamed the English countryside looking for rarities. Usually he'd find himself in the middle of all kinds of trouble which he'd have to resolve within the hour, and the BBC avoided almost all of the lechery and violence from the original books that the show was based on and instead focussed on cream cakes and cups of tea.

**Yoda from 'Star Wars'**

Voted the 25th greatest movie character of all time by Empire magazine, this small green creature of unknown species puts the Zen into the Star Wars universe, being both a fierce warrior and contemplative teacher. The puppet from the early film was voiced and controlled by Frank Oz but later Yoda became completely computer generated, the animators having to recreate some of the original 'mistakes' inherent in the physical puppet such as Yoda's ears tendency to wiggle when he talked.

**Miss Moneypenny from the Bond films and books**

Since the very first Bond film, Moneypenny has been in the background doing whatever it is she does, mostly spent flirting subtly with Bond during his fleeting moments in the office. It appears that she'll be forever single. The sexual tension between Moneypenny and Bond is almost entirely limited to the films; in Ian Fleming's books their relationship is strictly functional and the innuendo was added by the film makers to spice up their screen time together.

**Edna Mode from 'The Incredibles'**

Fashionista extraordinaire in this animated Pixar movie, Edna Mode is the diminutive bespectacled whirlwind behind the costumes for many members of the superhero community. Edna appeared alongside Pierce Brosnan at the 77th Academy Film Awards to present the award for costume design and is based on the legendary Hollywood costume designer Edith Head.

## Sherlock Holmes from the books by Sir Arthur Conan Doyle

It's not hard to argue that Sherlock Holmes is the most famous sleuth of all time, accompanied by his faithful Watson over many books and film adaptations, the most famous of all being 'The Hound Of The Baskervilles'. Although Sherlock Holmes only appeared in four full length novels he also appeared in fifty six short stories. Disappointingly, Holmes never actually said 'Elementary, my dear Watson' in any of the films or in any of Doyle's writing.

## Indiana Jones from 'Raiders Of The Lost Ark'

One of the greatest action heroes of all time, 'Indy' played by Harrison Ford was created by Steven Spielberg to bring 'Boys Own' adventure stories to the big screen in the early eighties. The first and best of the series, 'Raiders Of The Lost Ark' had Indiana Jones trying to get his hands on the lost Ark Of The Covenant before the Nazis could. Luckily he fails, and the Nazis get their comeuppance in one of the greatest (and finally most cryptic) movie endings ever.

## Atticus Finch from 'To Kill A Mockingbird'

This is author Harper Lee's only book, the fictional account of white lawyer Atticus Finch's difficult but ultimately successful attempt to represent black defendants in a criminal trial in Alabama during the Great Depression. The book, published in 1960 was an instant classic, winning the Pulitzer prize and inspiring generations of legal professionals. The film adaptation starring Gregory Peck as Atticus Finch won him the oscar for best actor in 1962.

# Zodiac Symbols

*Here's a list of the signs of the zodiac and their associated symbols, with a few tips on how to remember which is which*

## Capricorn

This symbol shows the horns of the goat, one horn turning into a wavy tail that indicates the mermaid end of the goat.

## Aquarius

Aquarius is represented by two wavy lines, one of top of the other. Of course these represent water.

## Pisces

The two arcs on each side can be seen as the faces of two fish coming together to kiss, the line being their mouths.

## Aries

The curly horns of the Ram are strongly represented in this symbol for Aries.

## Taurus

Like Aries, the horns of Taurus The Bull are the main symbolism in this symbol, albeit a lot straighter!

## Gemini

The roman numeral for the two twins is a fairly straightforward symbol.

## Cancer

The two sideways sixes in the symbol for cancer are often seen as the claws of the crab, or the crab's beady eyes.

## Leo

The mane of the Lion is represented here with this curly symbol.

## Virgo

This symbol is an M similar to Scorpio, but it appears to have crossed its legs. Like a virgin?

## Libra

The scales are quite obviously the symbolism for this Libra.

## Scorpio

This symbol is an M similar to Virgo, but with the single pointy tail of the scorpion at one end.

## Sagittarius

The arrow of the Centaur is simply represented in this symbol. You just need to remember that Sagittarius is an archer!

When you're trying to recall these symbols, it's a good idea to try and draw them too to get them firmly in your mind.

Here's a little exercise to see if you can remember each symbol, so grab a pen and get drawing!

1. Can you draw the symbol for Libra?
2. Can you draw the symbol for Virgo?
3. Can you draw the symbol for Aquarius?
4. Can you draw the symbol for Capricorn?
5. Can you draw the symbol for Sagittarius?
6. Can you draw the symbol for Taurus?
7. Can you draw the symbol for Aries?
8. Can you draw the symbol for Pisces?
9. Can you draw the symbol for Cancer?
10. Can you draw the symbol for Leo?
11. Can you draw the symbol for Scorpio?
12. Can you draw the symbol for Gemini?

Knowing the symbol for each star sign isn't essential but it's nice to know.

*Top Tip:* The flash cards are a great way to test yourself on the star sign symbols

See if you can incorporate the symbol for each sign into their visualisations. For instance, next time you think of Taurus The Bull and recall its mental image, try superimposing the symbol for Taurus onto the head of the bull. It's worth trying this for each sign because as you've probably learned by now, adding extra stuff to your mental pictures for each star sign isn't too difficult once you've started.

# Moving On

**What next?**

This book was never intended to be an exhaustive treatise on star signs and I'm hoping that learning this system has encouraged you to take things further. By now you should have a framework upon which you can hang almost any further knowledge. Should you find yourself delving into other books on the subject, try to visualise any new ideas you come across as vividly as possible and combine them with what you've already learned. Take the time to visualise and connect everything together and don't forget; what you can imagine, you can remember.

Good luck!

Julian Moore

# Registration Link

You can download the flash cards and audio by registering this product using the following link:

http://thecoldreadingcompany.co.uk/coldreading/ssflash

Once registered your details will be checked against your purchase and you will be sent an email with the download details.

*** NOTE: There is a very small chance that your email service provider might flag your registration email as spam. Should your email not arrive within an hour after registering please check your spam folder, making sure to mark the registration email as 'normal' mail (not spam) should it be there. This is to ensure that you don't miss any further updates from us.*

# Further Reading

**Other books in the 'Speed Learning' series
by Julian Moore**

Palmistry - Palm Readings In Your Own Words

Graphology - The Art Of Handwriting Analysis

Cartomancy - Fortune Telling With Playing Cards

The James Bond Cold Reading

Numerology - Numbers Past And Present With The Lo-Shu
Square

Don't forget to visit our website at
**www.thecoldreadingcompany.co.uk**

14732875R00058

Printed in Great Britain
by Amazon.co.uk, Ltd.,
Marston Gate.